CAMPAIGN 297

THE GEMPEI WAR 1180–85

The Great Samurai Civil War

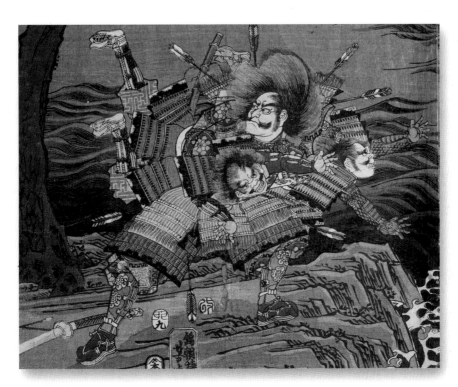

STEPHEN TURNBULL　　ILLUSTRATED BY GIUSEPPE RAVA

Series editor Marcus Cowper

First published in Great Britain in 2016 by Osprey Publishing,
PO Box 883, Oxford, OX1 9PL, UK
PO Box 3985, New York, NY 10185-3985, USA
E-mail: info@ospreypublishing.com

A CIP catalogue record for this book is available from the British Library.

ISBN: 978 1 4728 1384 8
PDF e-book ISBN: 978 1 4728 1385 5
e-Pub ISBN: 978 1 4728 1386 2

Editorial by Ilios Publishing Ltd, Oxford, UK (www.iliospublishing.com)
Index by Alan Rutter
Typeset in Myriad Pro and Sabon
Maps by Bounford.com
3D bird's-eye views by The Black Spot
Battlescene illustrations by Giuseppe Rava
Originated by PDQ Media, Bungay, UK
Printed in China through Worldprint Ltd.

16 17 18 19 20   10 9 8 7 6 5 4 3 2 1

ARTIST'S NOTE

Readers may care to note that the original paintings from which the colour
plates in this book were prepared are available for private sale. The
Publishers retain all reproduction copyright whatsoever. The artist can be
contacted via the following website:
www.g-rava.it
The Publishers regret that they can enter into no correspondence upon this
matter.

AUTHOR'S NOTE

The Gempei War, the great civil war of Japan, was named after the two rival
samurai clans called the Minamoto and the Taira. When their names are
pronounced in the Chinese style of Japanese orthography as 'Genji' and
'Heike' respectively and the first characters are combined, it produces the
compound 'Gempei', although modern written Japanese tends to use a
form of romanisation that leads to the compound 'Gem-pei' becoming
'Gen-pei'. It is as the Gempei War that the great conflict is best known, so
the traditional form will be retained here. For the further convenience of
readers the lunar dates used in the primary sources have been converted
to the Western calendar, and following conventional Japanese usage all
names are given with the surname first.

I have written about the Gempei War many times, but for this book I
have ignored all my previous work and gone back to the original Japanese
source materials combined with data drawn from observational visits to
each of the main battlefields involved. The reader may therefore be
confident that this is the most authoritative account of the Gempei War
currently available. All the pictures are my own except a few which are
gratefully acknowledged in the captions.

DEDICATION

The Gempei War 1180–85 is dedicated to my seventh grandchild, Sebastian
Turnbull, born on 24 July 2015.

THE WOODLAND TRUST

Osprey Publishing are supporting the Woodland Trust, the UK's leading
woodland conservation charity, by funding the dedication of trees.

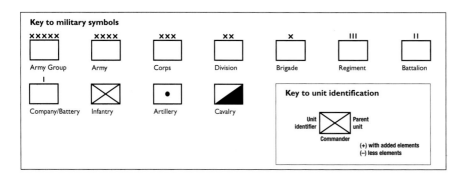

Key to military symbols

xxxxx	**xxxx**	**xxx**	**xx**	**x**	**III**	**II**
Army Group	Army	Corps	Division	Brigade	Regiment	Battalion
I	⊠	•	◣			
Company/Battery	Infantry	Artillery	Cavalry			

Key to unit identification

Unit identifier — Parent unit
Commander
(+) with added elements
(–) less elements

CONTENTS

INTRODUCTION

THE GEMPEI WAR IN JAPANESE CULTURE

The sound of the bell of Gionshōja echoes the impermanence of all things. The hue of the flowers of the teak tree declares that they who flourish must be brought low. Yea, the proud ones are but for a moment, like an evening dream in springtime. The mighty are destroyed at the last, they are but as the dust before the wind.

With these words begins *Heike Monogatari* (*The Tale of the Heike*), the great literary epic about Japan's Gempei War, where it is transformed into a dark romance. Unlike *Heike Monogatari*, it is the aim of the present work to provide a clear, concise and authoritative historical account of that great conflict, and although the emphasis will be on the war as a military campaign, the place of the Gempei War as a vitally important political and cultural phenomenon will not be overlooked. So far-reaching was its outcome in political terms that the Gempei War might be regarded not simply as a Japanese civil war but even as *the* Japanese civil war. Many other internal conflicts would take place over the following centuries but none, not even the decisive Sekigahara campaign of 1600, would bring about such a profound change in Japanese society as did the Gempei War. The battle of Sekigahara gave Japan a new ruling dynasty, but the Gempei War had already given Japan a new form of rule. It had created a situation whereby Japan was no longer governed by an imperial bureaucracy under the emperor but by a military aristocracy drawn from the samurai class whose rule was exercised through the Shogun, Japan's military dictator. By means of the Gempei War the samurai displaced the imperial court and entered the mainstream of Japanese political life, a position they were to hold until the emergence of modern Japan in 1868.

The political consequences of the Gempei War were therefore substantial, but it also had many lasting cultural influences through its effects on the samurai, both in terms of how they were perceived and what future samurai would do. Through art and literature the Gempei War provided successive generations of Japanese warriors with a reference point from which to draw most of what became known as the samurai tradition. *Heike Monogatari*, which relates the story of the Gempei War as a drama of fate and retribution inflicted upon the Taira family, will be widely quoted in this book. Woodblock prints and scrolls showing the heroes of the Gempei War will provide many of the illustrations, and reference will also be made to the vivid retelling of these stories within Japan's classical Noh theatre. There are more plots in the Noh dramas based on the Gempei War than on any other period of Japanese history, and over one in ten of all Noh plays are based on incidents related in *Heike Monogatari* alone. In a typical play the spirit of a dead warrior appears and re-enacts in some way his tragic death on a battlefield of the Gempei War, drawing from and adding to the magic and mystique of this great conflict.

Further evidence for the war's historical and cultural importance is contained within the more mundane accounts of later battles and wars, where challenges to combat and deeds of daring are often recorded with reference to the supposed golden age of samurai heroics that the Gempei War provided. In the citing of such precedents the events of the Gempei War eclipse much of what went before it and even more of what came after. In many cases those accounts refer to heroic ancestors whose exploits their descendants now wished to emulate. These glorious and much-exaggerated deeds included brave challenges to individual combat, noble acts of honourable suicide, distinguished feats of arms with bow or sword and even the basic underlying concept of loyalty to the point of death. Key examples of these principles would be identified within the course of Japan's greatest civil war, and some include the first occurrence of certain archetypal samurai accomplishments and virtues. These details, reinforced by plays, poems and epic literature, would eventually provide the foundations for bushidō, the 'way of the warrior' that was to be manipulated and used by successive modern Japanese governments. Bushidō would inspire and sustain Japanese troops in their overseas expeditions from the 1890s onwards, so it is no exaggeration to state that the Gempei War was still influencing Japanese fighting men during the wars of the 20th century.

As well as setting out the strategic and tactical details of the war's many campaigns, this book will attempt to show the cruel reality of 12th-century Japanese warfare, which went far beyond the heroics in *Heike Monogatari*.

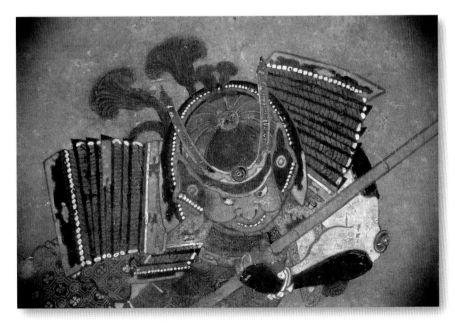

The Gempei War was the conflict whereby the warrior aristocracy known as the samurai took over the governance of Japan. In this detail from a painted scroll we see the grinning face of a samurai warrior clutching his bow. His head is bent down so that his helmet acts as a shield against the arrows loosed at him.

To do this I will make extensive use of two very different sources. The first is *Azuma Kagami* (*Mirror of Eastern Japan*) which is an official history of Japan written in diary form and compiled sometime after 1266, the last date included in the work. *Azuma Kagami*, which includes transcripts of official papers, provides a chronological record of the Gempei War and has much valuable information about the background to the small-scale heroics that it also describes. From *Azuma Kagami* one can tease out the overall aims of a campaign and follow the major tactical moves of battles. The second source is the above-mentioned *Heike Monogatari*, the greatest of the literary genre known as *gunkimono* (war tales). It was compiled somewhat later than *Azuma Kagami*. There are many descriptions of brave individual exploits and single combats, all of which played a role in the achievement of victory, but here and there are also some very believable accounts of ambushes, arson attacks and massacres that place the heroic deeds in their proper context. When combined with the *Azuma Kagami* material, it will provide for the first time in the English language a complete picture of Japan's greatest civil war.

THE STRATEGIC SITUATION

Heike Monogatari presents the Gempei War as a drama dominated by named samurai and their acts of glory, but the reality of the situation was far more complex than the great epic implies. The fighting was not just a series of individual achievements and even the name 'Gempei War' disguises the true identity of the combatants. The Minamoto clan were indeed the eventual victors and the Taira clan were effectively annihilated, but many other family names such as Fujiwara, Sasaki, Satake and Ashikaga are mentioned in the accounts of the fighting. In some cases their adoption of the names Minamoto and Taira merely indicated their support for local factions in the struggle rather than actual membership of rival clans. In those situations the names were little more than convenient labels assumed by participants who desired to gain some advantage from their affiliation. When the Minamoto eventually

Minamoto Yoshitsune and Benkei at the battle of Yashima in 1185, from a painted screen in the Watanabe Museum, Tottori.

6

Japan at the time of the Gempei War, 1180–85.

CHINA

Hokkaidō

Sea of Japan

KOREA

JAPAN

Honshū

DEWA

⑤
Hiraizumi

SADO

MUTSU

NOTO

ECHIGO

⑥ ETCHU

SHIMOTSUKE

KAGA

⑩

KŌZUKE

HIDA

SHINANO

HITACHI

WAKASA

ECHIZEN

MUSASHI

TAJIMA

TANGO

MINO

KAI

SHIMŌSA

HOKI

INABA

Lake Biwa

ŌMI

OWARI

SURUGA

SAGAMI

KAZUSA

IZUMO

MIMASAKA

TAMBA

Kyoto

MIKAWA

IZU

AWA

IWAMI

BINGO

BIZEN

HARIMA

② ④

SETTSU

⑦

③

IGA

⑧

TOTOMI

Kamakura

AKI

BITCHU

IZUMI

ISE

①

SANUKI

⑨

AWAJI

YAMATO

SHIMA

NAGATO

SUO

YAMASHIRO

KAWACHI

CHIKUZEN

BUZEN

Inland Sea

IYO

TOSA

KII

HIZEN

CHIKUGO

BUNGO

Shikoku

HIGO

Kyushu

SATSUMA

HYUGA

PACIFIC OCEAN

OSUMI

N

Battles
1. Dannoura (1185)
2. Fujigawa (1180)
3. Ichinotani (1184)
4. Ishibashiyama (1180)
5. Koromogawa (1189)
6. Kurikara (1183)
7. Mizushima (1183)
8. Uji (1180 and 1184)
9. Yashima (1185)
10. Yokotagawara (1181)

0	200 miles
0	200km

triumphed it was not as the result of winning a fight between two families; it was instead the favourable outcome of a complex national civil war.

In a further complication, much of the fighting by the Minamoto was not conducted against Taira supporters but against rivals within their own clan. In particular, the main campaigns of 1183 and 1184 were directed against Kiso Yoshinaka, whose sphere of influence had begun to overlap with his cousin Yoritomo. Finally, the fighting during the Gempei War was by no means continuous. It consisted instead of a series of small-scale operations that built up slowly towards a crushing and decisive climax, and no fighting took place for most of 1182, when famine devastated Japan.

The two families of Minamoto and Taira were nevertheless the nuclei around which the war took place, and when the Gempei War began in 1180 their rivalry was personified by the chief protagonists: Minamoto Yoritomo (1147–99) and Taira Kiyomori (1118–81), two men who were separated by a large geographical distance and an even greater social one. In the year 1180 Minamoto Yoritomo was a most unlikely future victor, being geographically remote from the centre of power. He was living in exile in eastern Japan in Izu province, one of the places to which the remnants of his family had been banished following their defeat in an earlier uprising against the Taira. Eastern Japan contained the Minamoto heartlands, making the eventual Gempei War very much an east–west split.

The rise of the Taira
In 1180 Yoritomo's rivals in the Taira family looked unassailable. They were physically located around the vital imperial capital of Kyoto and were completely enmeshed in the government of Japan, with their main supporters enjoying lands and possessions in western Japan around the Inland Sea. As a seagoing clan the Taira had established a formidable reputation for controlling piracy, but their political position at the start of the Gempei War had also been helped by a series of dynastic marriages, the suppression of two rebellions and above all by the dominant personality of their leader Taira Kiyomori. Among his other accomplishments Kiyomori had managed to control the militant Buddhist monks whose private armies often intimidated the religiously sensitive imperial court. He had also managed to manipulate the

Taira Kiyomori as a young man. Taira Kiyomori took his family to the pinnacle of their achievements, and even though he is best remembered as a great statesman (or tyrant), Kiyomori had an earlier career as a very successful samurai warrior. Here he is shown in the costume of an archer holding the bow that was the mark of a samurai.

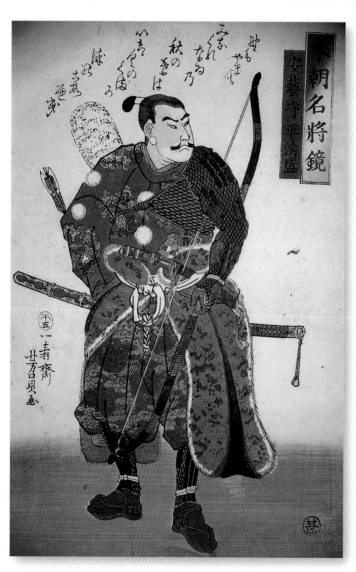

complicated system then in vogue whereby reigning emperors would retire, become Buddhist priests and continue to rule behind the scenes as *hōō*, retired or 'cloistered' emperors. The Taira had also infiltrated the closest ranks of the imperial court by giving daughters in marriage and had managed to supplant the Fujiwara family in this practice by 1180.

Kiyomori's earlier military campaigns had successfully eliminated any other samurai rivals who sought to emulate his success, although at that stage the division had not been a simple one of choosing between the Minamoto and the Taira. In the 1156 Hōgen Rebellion, which was caused by an imperial succession dispute, prominent members of the Minamoto and Taira clans had taken part on both sides. During that brief disturbance Minamoto Tameyoshi (1096–1156) and his son Tametomo (1139–70), a samurai renowned for his archery, found themselves opposing Tameyoshi's other son Yoshitomo (1123–60), who was allied with Taira Kiyomori. The fighting involved a night attack that concluded when the besieged building was set on fire. Minamoto Tameyoshi was defeated and executed, and his son Tametomo was banished. In 1160 a similar uprising called the Heiji Rebellion was carried out on behalf of two more rival imperial claimants, but this time Taira samurai fought Minamoto in a very clear division of loyalties. Minamoto Yoshitomo, the former supporter of Taira Kiyomori, led an attack on the Sanjō Palace in Kyoto, but Kiyomori defeated him so severely that the Minamoto had to flee for their lives. Yoshitomo was eventually tracked down and killed, and to complete his triumph Kiyomori ordered the execution of all the Minamoto supporters who had challenged him. Out of the main branch of the family only a handful of very old or very young members were spared or exiled. One of them was Minamoto Yoritomo.

As may be expected, the defeated Minamoto had been labelled rebels to the throne, and when they had been safely banished or eliminated, Taira Kiyomori, the loyal queller of the rebels, went from strength to strength as the official protector of the legitimate emperor. In 1160 Kiyomori became the first samurai to be made a *kugyō* (senior nobleman), and in 1161 his programme of marriage alliances bore its first fruits when his niece gave birth to Prince Norihito. In 1167 Kiyomori was given the title of *Daijō Daijin* (Chancellor), the highest rank that an emperor could award, and in the following year of 1168 7-year-old Prince Norihito ascended the throne as Emperor Takakura. So strong was Kiyomori's position that his great-nephew was appointed over the head of an elder non-Taira half-brother called Prince Mochihito (1151– 80). He was the son of Kiyomori's greatest political rival, the Cloistered Emperor Go-Shirakawa (literally 'Shirakawa the Second' 1127–92), who had tried to rule behind the scenes but had been upstaged by the Taira.

Taira Kiyomori's intelligence network was also considerable. It ensured that any potential rebels could be summarily dealt with even before they had a chance to act, as was shown by the rapid and firm treatment dealt out to the leaders of the Shishigatani conspiracy in 1177. The planners were acting in support of Go-Shirakawa, but they were arrested and exiled before they could move into action. The following year Kiyomori placed Go-Shirakawa under house arrest, and early in 1180 he pulled off his greatest political coup. He now had a 2-year-old grandson, so the reigning Emperor Takakura, who was still only 9 years old, was gently persuaded to retire to make room for the new Emperor Antoku. Not surprisingly, Antoku's succession was challenged by Go-Shirakawa's son Prince Mochihito, who had now been passed over twice, although Mochihito's challenge to the Taira was not merely a personal grudge. It encompassed and distilled a widespread and growing opposition to the Taira monopoly of court politics, and was easily manipulated by pro-Minamoto sympathisers. Kiyomori had antagonised many people through his own efforts and through the deputies he had appointed out in the provinces, who ruled with little reference to the well-established and often pro-Minamoto local lords. Mochihito therefore became a useful figurehead for their discontent, and the cynical means by which his personal grievance was converted into a national rebellion became the conflict now known as the Gempei War.

The eastern warriors

It is important to note at this stage that throughout the time of the Taira ascendancy there had been no question of them establishing a new regime to challenge the accepted imperial hegemony. Instead Kiyomori had operated within the existing system according to the prevailing rules of patronage and influence. He had brought his family to a position of pre-eminence not by asserting a new form of power but by accepting an old one. The Taira rule was Kyoto-based, emperor-focussed and, according to every established norm, employed a methodology that had displayed great loyalty towards everything that Japan stood for. Yet in this close attention to the status quo the rise of the Taira revealed an underlying weakness that was eventually to cost them dear, because in concentrating so totally on central government Kiyomori had neglected to build up support among the provincial warriors of the east. These men may have been geographically remote from the imperial court, but they had grown rich and powerful from the rewards heaped upon them by a succession of grateful emperors whose cause they had served by pushing forward the boundaries of imperial government in remote areas of Japan and suppressing bandits and rebels. The Hōgen and Heiji rebellions had shown how disadvantaged these provincial warriors were when they attempted to muscle in on the Kyoto establishment. On those occasions they had been overcome both politically and militarily by Taira Kiyomori, but instead of simply admitting defeat, their members, who included most crucially the Minamoto children generously spared by Kiyomori after Heiji, had chosen to build up their own power bases in the distant regions. The only response made by the Taira was to attempt to control them through unpopular local deputies, which had made matters worse. That was the situation in which young Minamoto Yoritomo found himself, and in 1180 he received a copy of Prince Mochihito's declaration of war against the Taira.

This painted scroll depicts a mounted samurai wearing a *horo*, the curious 'arrow catcher' made from a cloth spread over a bamboo framework that indicated an elite warrior. Judging by the fact that he is tightening the girth on his saddle, he is probably Kajiwara Kagesue at the second battle of Uji in 1184.

CHRONOLOGY

The Gempei War may be conveniently divided into three phases:

1180–82   Taira success in the Kyoto area is followed by Minamoto success in the east; a period of stalemate is then caused by an extensive famine.

1183–84   Minamoto Yoshinaka defeats the Taira but is then overthrown by Minamoto cousins.

1184–85   The Taira are destroyed in a succession of campaigns led by Minamoto Yoshitsune.

The detailed chronology is as follows:

1156   The Hōgen Rebellion.

1160   The Heiji Rebellion.

1168   Accession of Emperor Takakura, Taira Kiyomori's nephew.

1177   The Shishigatani conspiracy is crushed.

The Gempei War:

1180

18 March   Abdication of Emperor Takakura.

5 May   Prince Mochihito's proclamation is issued.

18 May   Accession of Emperor Antoku, Taira Kiyomori's grandson.

20 June   Minamoto Yorimasa is defeated at the first battle of Uji.

8 September   Minamoto Yoritomo defeats Taira Kanetaka at Yamagi in Izu province.

14 September   Yoritomo is defeated at the battle of Ishibashiyama.

19 September   Yoritomo flees by sea to Awa province.

20 October   The Taira army leaves Kyoto to challenge Yoritomo.

26 October   Yoritomo arrives in Kamakura.

9 November   The battle of Fujigawa.

10 November   Minamoto Yoshitsune joins Yoritomo.

19 November   The retreating Taira re-enter Kyoto.

5 December   Yoritomo establishes the *Samurai-dokoro* (Samurai Office).

19 December   Revolts in Ōmi and Mino provinces are crushed by Taira Tomomori.

1181

15 January   Taira Shigehira burns Nara.

20 March   Death of Taira Kiyomori.

25 April   The battle of Sunomata.

27 July   The battle of Yokotagawara.

November   The Taira temporarily pacify Kyūshū.

1182

The Great Famine halts all hostilities

1183

20 May	The battle of Hiuchijō.
24 May	The battle of Ataka.
31 May	The battle of Hannyano.
2 June	The battle of Kurikara.
22 June	The battle of Shinowara.
11 August	Yoshinaka enters the Enryaku-ji monastery.
17 August	The Taira abandon Kyoto.
17 November	The battle of Mizushima; the battle of Muroyama.

1184

1 January	The battle of the Hōjūji Palace.
3 March	Second battle of Uji; death of Yoshinaka at Awazu.
13 March	Yoshitsune and Noriyori advance from Kyoto against the Taira.
18 March	The battle of Mikusayama.
20 March	The battle of Ichinotani.
7 September	Noriyori leaves Kamakura.
6 October	Noriyori arrives in Kyoto.

1185

10 January	The battle of Kojima (Fujito).
22/24 March	The battle of Yashima.
25 April	The battle of Dannoura.

Aftermath:

1189

15 June	The battle of Koromogawa.

1192

Yoritomo becomes Shogun.

1199

The death of Yoritomo.

OPPOSING COMMANDERS

THE MINAMOTO LEADERS

Several important names appear within the upper echelons of command during the Gempei War. All seem to flourish for a while until death, disgrace or politics removes them from the scene. In the case of the Minamoto family there are three key individuals to consider: Yoritomo, Yoshinaka and Yoshitsune, whose military careers fit quite neatly into the three phases of the war. The other Minamoto generals – Yorimasa, Yukiie and Noriyori – have important roles to play, but each is overshadowed by the leading figures in their campaigns.

Minamoto Yoritomo (1147–99), the eventual victor in the Gempei War, is remembered in Japanese history as a statesman, not as a soldier. He was a boy at the time of the Heiji Rebellion and was exiled to Izu province. During his 20-year-long sojourn there Yoritomo was officially under the supervision of two local lords. The first was Itō Sukechika, whose touch was light, largely owing to the fact that he spent most of his time in Kyoto. Yoritomo took advantage of this and fathered a child by Sukechika's daughter Yaehime. His other guardian Hōjō Tokimasa provided Yoritomo with a wife, the redoubtable Masako, who would be a tower of strength to the Minamoto in later years. Legend has it that sometime during his time of exile Yoritomo was visited by a wandering priest called Mongaku, who presented him with the skull of his father Yoshitomo, thereby provoking him into action against the Taira, but it was the receipt on 23 May 1180 of Prince Mochihito's proclamation that provided the real stimulus for his actions. Yet it is not as a general that Yoritomo then reveals himself. During his first victory of the war Yoritomo stayed behind and prayed while his troops fought. At his second battle he was defeated and fled, only to return for a freak victory. From this time on he becomes the ruler of the Minamoto who dispatches troops to fight the Taira in distant provinces rather than a commander on the battlefield.

In this *ema* (prayer board) from the Otonashi Shrine in Itō (Shizuoka Prefecture) we see the young Minamoto Yoritomo, the victor in the Gempei War and Japan's first Shogun. As a youth he was exiled to this area and formed a liaison with Yaehime, the daughter of his guardian, who is also shown on the *ema*. They are enshrined at the Otonashi Shrine.

Minamoto Yorimasa (1104–80) had survived the Heiji Rebellion and was living a quiet life as virtually the only Minamoto in an imperial court totally dominated by the Taira. He was renowned both as a samurai and as a poet, and was much in favour in the imperial court, having once supposedly killed with an arrow a monster that was terrorising the palace. Like Taira Kiyomori, Yorimasa had also stood up to the warrior monks and had earned their admiration when he showed great respect to the *mikoshi*, the sacred palanquin in which the *kami* (deity) was believed to dwell, when he fought them in battle. He would become the first to rebel against the Taira.

Kiso Yoshinaka (1154–84) was Yoritomo's cousin, and like him was exiled at a young age. In his case the banishment was to Kiso in the mountains of Shinano province, hence the name by which he is better known. His military career would be brief and spectacular, exploding like a sky rocket and then falling to earth. He received Prince Mochihito's proclamation in 1180 and acted upon it within his local area very much as Yoritomo had done, supported by his uncle Yukiie. Yoshinaka led all his campaigns personally and was so successful in 1183 that he alarmed Yoritomo as much as he did the Taira. As a result we will read of Kiso Yoshinaka fighting against the Minamoto as well as the Taira.

Minamoto Yoshitsune (1159–89), the younger brother of Yoritomo, is one of the most famous samurai commanders in the whole of Japanese history. In spite of being short in stature and of unremarkable physique, he inspired his followers to three celebrated victories that brought the Gempei War to a successful conclusion. Legend has embellished much of his life. He is said to have been taught sword fighting by the *tengu* (goblins) of the forests, and is famous for having defeated the giant monk Benkei, who became his faithful follower. Minamoto Yoshitsune's reputation as a samurai commander, however, is much more soundly based and well deserved, and the final phase of the war is almost all his, although the important contribution of his brother Noriyori will be acknowledged in the pages that follow.

LEFT
Minamoto Yorimasa was the first Minamoto leader to go to war following Prince Mochihito's proclamation of rebellion against the Taira. Yorimasa was a noted poet and had always been in favour at court since he had rid the palace of a strange monster that was haunting it. That is the scene depicted in this print by Yoshitoshi, where Yorimasa is shown in court costume as a palace guard.

RIGHT
Benkei was a warrior monk from Miidera who became the faithful follower and bodyguard of Minamoto Yoshitsune. In this statue of him on the coast of Hokkaidō he is dressed in typical warrior-monk garb, with a head cowl, prayer beads, *geta* (wooden clogs) and carrying a *naginata* (glaive).

THE TAIRA LEADERS

By comparison with the Minamoto commanders, the Taira leaders lack personality and individual character. In peacetime their great leader was **Kiyomori** (1118–81), and as the above summary of his career indicates, by 1180 he had made the transition from general to statesman that Yoritomo would later copy. Nevertheless, the fighting and leadership skills he had demonstrated during the Hōgen and Heiji rebellions show that he was a samurai leader, and in another famous encounter as a young man he had

Taira Kiyomori made many enemies among the established Buddhist and Shintō priesthoods when he lavished attention on his shrine of Itsukushima on the Inland Sea at the expense of the ancient foundations of Kyoto and Nara. Here he is mocked satirically as ordering the sun to stand still in the heavens so that the building work could continue.

dared to loose an arrow at the *mikoshi* of the warrior monks, in contrast to the respect shown by Minamoto Yorimasa. His antipathy to militant Buddhism disguised his own deep religious commitment, which found chief expression in his endowment of the shrine of Itsukushima on the Inland Sea. Its position in Taira territory further antagonised the Buddhist establishment around Kyoto and Nara, and stories grew of Kiyomori trying to command the sun to stand still in the heavens so that work could continue on his precious shrine. Kiyomori therefore entered the Gempei War with sworn enemies among the Buddhist hierarchy as well as the Minamoto.

Kiyomori's heir Shigemori died in 1179, so the leader of the Taira who followed Kiyomori was **Munemori** (1147–85). He had none of his father's political skill and little of his military capacity; in fact Munemori would be blamed for the family's eventual defeat. The antagonism against him was such that at Dannoura his own mother exposed him as the son not of the great Kiyomori but the offspring of an umbrella merchant, smuggled into the palace at birth to replace an unwanted baby daughter. With the hapless Munemori at the helm, it was fortunate for the Taira family that he had brothers and nephews who could fight, and his brother **Tomomori** (1152–85) was the finest of them all. His name will appear in the accounts of some of the key battles of the Gempei War, where he displays the finest traditions of samurai generalship. Indeed, it is really only when Tomomori is in action that we find the Taira victorious. He was present at Ichinotani and Yashima, and was instrumental in extracting the Taira from their reverses. Tomomori was ably supported in the later campaigns by Taira Noritsune (1160–85).

In terms of his personality and character **Shigehira** (1158–85), another son of Kiyomori, is the Taira's equivalent of the Minamoto's Yoshinaka. Excoriated for his destruction of the temples of Nara, an operation that went far beyond what was necessary, Shigehira added greatly to the enmity for the Taira that came from the religious establishment. He was captured at Ichinotani and executed. Taira Tadanori was another victim at Ichinotani. **Taira Koremori** (1158–84) was Kiyomori's grandson, and is best remembered for being the loser at the supposed 'non-battle' of the Fujigawa in 1180. He led the equally disastrous expedition against Yoshinaka in 1183, and when the Taira finally retreated to Yashima, Koremori spread a rumour that he had drowned. He then slipped away to become a monk on the holy mountain of Kōyasan.

Taira Tomomori was the finest of all the Taira generals. He took part in most of their major battles and died at Dannoura. This painted scroll of him in court costume hangs in the museum of the Akamagū at Dannoura.

OPPOSING FORCES

The Gempei War may have been a revolution in terms of its eventual outcome, but there was nothing revolutionary about the way the war was conducted because its strategy, tactics and weaponry were stuck in the technology of samurai warfare that had already been developing since the Gosannen War of the 11th century. Even though the exploits carried out during the Gempei War would provide Japanese culture with archetypal stories about military behaviour, they are still limited to the use of bows, horses and edged weapons. The Gempei War was certainly not a military revolution.

ARMS AND ARMOUR

This long continuity is best illustrated by the relatively unchanged visual image that the samurai presents over a period of about 200 years, which is of an aristocratic warrior holding a bow, mounted on a horse and dressed in a style of armour known as a *yoroi*. The armour will be dealt with first, because its design influenced how the samurai fought. At first sight a typical *yoroi* armour looks like a very colourful, elaborate and even flimsy version of anything that could be called a suit of armour. It was put together from several different sections made not from large solid plates or chain mail in the European style but from a number of small scales tied together and lacquered to weatherproof them. Rows of these scales were combined into strong yet flexible armour plates by binding them together with silk or leather cords. This style of armour construction was common throughout much of East Asia. Each scale was made of iron or leather, and because a suit made entirely from iron would be far too heavy to wear,

The style of samurai armour worn during the Gempei War was the same as that shown here on a painted scroll depicting the Gosannen War of the 11th century. Note the bearskin boots and the wooden reel used for carrying a spare bowstring.

the iron scales were concentrated in the areas that needed most protection and otherwise alternated with the lighter leather scales. The samurai's *yoroi* was derived from a simpler early type which continued in use during the Gempei War as the armour worn by foot soldiers, whose unadorned wrap-around style was called a *dō maru*, of which a variant opening at the back rather than at the sides was called a *haramaki*. By contrast the developed samurai *yoroi* was sturdier and provided good protection for the body for an overall weight of about 30kg. The main disadvantage of the *yoroi* was not its weight but its rigid box-like design, which restricted the samurai's movements when he was dismounted or using hand weapons from the saddle.

This helmet preserved at Kuramadera in Kyoto is said to have belonged to Minamoto Yoshitsune. Famous warriors often donated armour to shrines and temples so the attribution is quite likely. It is also of typical 12th-century construction, being made from riveted plates around a central hole.

This magnificent reproduction helmet is a fine copy of those worn in the Gempei War. Note the *fukigayeshi* (turnbacks) on the *shikoro* (neck guard), the grinning devil face frontlet and the long golden *kuwagata* ('antlers'). (Royal Armouries Museum, Leeds)

The colours of the dyed silk cords gave a brilliance to this classic design, of which the body of the armour, the *dō*, consisted of four sections held together by a belt. The right side panel was put on first, then the other three, which were already fastened together. Two small guards were attached to the shoulder straps to prevent the tying cords from being cut, and a sheet of ornamented leather acted as a breastplate. Two large shoulder plates, the *sode*, were tied to the shoulder straps. They were then attached loosely to the rear of the armour by a large ornamental bow called the *agemaki*. The *agemaki* allowed the arms free movement while keeping the body covered by the shield-like *sode*. The heavy iron *kabuto* (helmet) provided a solid protection for the head. Helmets were made from separate iron plates fastened together with large projecting conical rivets. A peak, the *mabisashi*, was riveted onto the front and covered with patterned leather, while the neck was protected by a wide and heavy five-piece neck guard called a *shikoro*, which hung from the bowl. The top four plates of the *shikoro* were folded back at the front to form the *fukigayeshi* (turnbacks), which stopped downward cuts aimed at the horizontal lacing of the *shikoro*. Normally an *eboshi* (cap) was worn under the helmet as padding, but if the samurai's hair was very long his *motodori* (pigtail) was allowed to pass through the *tehen*, the hole in the centre of the helmet's crown where the plates met. No armour was worn on the right arm to leave it free for drawing the bow, but a simple bag-like sleeve (*kote*) with sewn-on plates was worn on the left arm.

This highly detailed print provides an excellent illustration of the typical *yoroi* armour worn by a samurai in the Gempei War. The way that the *yoroi* hung round the samurai's body is very well indicated.

THE MOUNTED ARCHER

Of all the weapons wielded on the Gempei battlefields none was more highly regarded than the *yumi*, the Japanese longbow. Popular culture may laud the famous samurai sword for being the 'soul of the samurai', but that concept and the expression itself lay a few centuries into the future, and a passage in *Konjaku Monogatari* provides a surprise for anyone brought up with the tradition of the sword's priority over the bow. One night robbers attacked Tachibana Norimitsu while he was on his way to visit a female acquaintance. He was armed only with a sword, and 'Norimitsu crouched down and looked around, but as he could not see any sign of a bow, but only a great glittering sword, he thought with relief, "It's not a bow at any rate."' Norimitsu did in fact vanquish the robbers, but his evident relief that he was not up against

Taira Shigemori, who predeceased his father Kiyomori, is the subject of this lively print showing a mounted samurai in action. Arrows are whizzing around him. Note how the various layers of the *yoroi* compress to afford greater protection.

anyone armed with a bow is very telling. A bow in the hands of a skilled archer, which is what all elite samurai were trained to be, gave him a considerable advantage over a swordsman who could be incapacitated before he came within striking distance.

The other element that made up the ideal warrior in the Gempei War was the ownership and use of a horse. A samurai was most appreciated for his skills in *kyūba no michi* (the way of bow and horse), although the great emphasis upon mounted warfare within the *gunkimono* reflects the aristocratic make-up of the target audience for these literary works rather than any strict historical reality. The impression is therefore given that all samurai were mounted warriors. However, the comparative realism shown on painted scrolls such as *Heiji Monogatari emaki* restores the balance to provide a much better idea of the composition of a typical army. On these illustrations we always see some mounted archers who fit the profile of elite samurai. They are attended by simply armed foot soldiers, most of whom are acting in the capacity of servants, weapon carriers and grooms. Other foot soldiers in action around them are infantrymen recruited or press-ganged into service, but there is also an intermediate type who appear to be 'foot samurai'. These men are of rough appearance, which is usually indicated by giving them beards and bare feet, even though they are wearing what appears to be full *yoroi* armour. Unlike their mounted superiors, they are carrying *naginata* (glaives), which had shafts of an oval cross section to aid the grip and bore fierce sword-like curved blades. It is therefore clear from illustrations like these that a simple division between mounted samurai archers and lower-class foot soldiers is not sufficient to describe a samurai army of the Gempei War. Instead, in any typical battle there is a class gradation that reflects the social origins and wealth of the participants. Nor was dismounted warfare taboo to the wealthy; even generals had to fight on foot under certain conditions. One example is ship-board warfare, but still we see a preference for the bow until they come to close quarters, draw their swords and engage each other hand to hand. In other encounters awkward mountainous terrain and bad weather conditions such as at the battle of Ishibashiyama in 1180 would demand an entirely dismounted force.

The type of bow employed during the Gempei War was very similar to the ones used today in the martial art of *kyūdō*. They were made from deciduous wood backed with bamboo on the side furthest from the archer. The rattan binding wound round the body of the bow reinforced the poor adhesive qualities of the glue used to fasten the sections together, and the whole bow was lacquered to weatherproof it. The arrows were made from the straightest possible bamboo. The nock was cut just above a node for strength, and three feathers were fitted to the shaft. Bowstrings were made of plant fibre, usually hemp

In this section from a copy of *Heiji Monogatari emaki* in Okayama Prefectural Museum we see the intermediate 'foot samurai' who are depicted as rough characters with beards and bare feet in spite of their ornate *yoroi* armour. They are carrying *naginata*.

or ramie, coated with wax to give a hard, smooth surface. A modern bow reflects the origins of the *yumi* as a mounted archer's weapon because it is loosed from one-third of the way up its length. At this point on the bow there is a reinforced handgrip. Just as the modern *kyūdō* archer lifts the bow and lowers it to his cheek, so did the Gempei War samurai hold the bow above his head to clear the horse, and then move his hands apart as the bow was brought down to end with the left arm straight and the right hand held steady near the right ear.

For all its length the Japanese longbow had nothing like the power of the bows wielded by the mounted warriors from the steppes of Central Asia. The maximum effective range of a Japanese arrow was unlikely to be more than about 20m, and the preferred distance for inflicting a wound or killing an opponent through a weak point in his armour was little more than 10m. The *yumi* was therefore essentially a close-combat weapon and the mounted

Yabusame is the martial art derived from the mounted archery of the Gempei War period. The close range at which the target is struck here at Nikkō is probably little different from the use of the bow from horseback in a combat situation, where close-range archery was the norm.

archer had to gallop up quite close to his opponent in order to engage him, as is made clear in several accounts. Furthermore, his human target did not usually remain static, and was no doubt trying to kill the attacker at the same time. An added complication was provided by the box-like design of the *yoroi*, which meant that the angle of fire of a bow was considerably restricted. The archer could only shoot to his left side along an arc of about 45 degrees from about 'nine o'clock' to 'eleven o'clock' relative to the forward direction of movement; the horse's neck prevented any closer angle firing. The unevenly balanced *yoroi* was also not a tight fit around the body, leaving it free to swing from side to side and upset the archer's equilibrium. Accuracy could be improved from time spent hunting and hours of practice on ranges where the arrows were discharged at small wooden targets while the horse was galloping along. This became the traditional martial art of *yabusame*, which is still performed at some Japanese festivals nowadays. The *yabusame* archer, dressed in traditional hunting gear, discharges the bow at right angles to his direction of movement, but even in *yabusame* the bow is loosed very close to its target. In terms of weapon efficiency, to fight dismounted may even have given the elite mounted archer an advantage when it came to the accuracy and power of his bow.

THE SAMURAI IN BATTLE

The essence of the mounted archer's role was to be an individual marksman. Every arrow was meant for an honourable opponent, and much exaggerated ritual was derived from this ideal. Traditionally a battle would begin by the firing of signal arrows high into the air over the enemy lines. Each signal arrow had a large, bulblike perforated wooden head which whistled as it flew through the air. The sound was a call to the gods to draw their attention to the great deeds of bravery which were about to be performed by the rival warriors. There would then be one or more feats of individual combat which

When a samurai was unhorsed, as in this example from a painted screen showing the battle of Ichinotani (1184), his bow would be discarded in favour of the *tachi* (sword) slung at his side.

would be fought in the area between the two armies. This ritual was traditionally and eagerly expected, and *Heike Monogatari* gives the impression that they were exclusively individual encounters between worthy opponents who sought out each other by issuing a verbal challenge that involved reciting their exploits and their pedigrees. The challenge would be answered from within the opposing army, thus providing a recognised mechanism whereby only worthy opponents would meet in combat.

Such personal encounters were called *ikki uchi* (single mounted warrior combats) and certainly did occur. But once the two armies had clashed, it is unlikely that individual challenges like these could continue to have been issued and responded to, and there are in fact very few examples in the *gunkimono* where elaborate declarations are recorded at this stage in the proceedings, although some took place after one side had admitted defeat. Because of the obvious difficulties of being able to conduct verbal negotiations above the din of battle, a more likely scenario is that when entering a wholesale battle situation the samurai shouted out their names as war cries to proclaim general, rather than specific challenges.

Carefully chosen examples of these single combats will be included in the narratives which follow. Typically they would start with an exchange of arrows from charging horses, then proceed to edged weapons and sometimes they would end with bare hands. Swords would be drawn when the samurai ran out of arrows or otherwise lost the use of their bows, so prowess with cutting weapons was vital. At this point the samurai sword came into its own, and around the time of the Gempei War the technology of sword-making was reaching its point of technical perfection. A sword was forged from iron sand to make a billet of steel, which was folded and beaten numerous times to produce a blade that consisted of thousands of very strong microscopic layers. Most swords were also of dual composition, whereby the harder section that would take the cutting edge was cushioned within a surrounding body of softer, springier steel. When quenched and honed, the sword's blade was sharp and its body both strong and resilient, so that when it was wielded in the classic two-handed fashion, it could be made to deflect an attacking weapon before the samurai moved in for the kill.

The longer sword of the two usually carried by samurai in this early period was called a *tachi* and was slung from a separate sword belt with the cutting edge downwards. The *tachi* was the samurai's principle sidearm, but a sword with a much shorter blade was also at his side. The combination we see being worn on picture

It was not easy to wield the normally two-handed *tachi* from the back of a horse. The one advantage the horseman had was that his superior position would enable him to hit a foot soldier with greater force. On this painted screen a samurai is using his sword like this at the battle of Yashima.

scrolls such as *Heiji Monogatari emaki* are of a *tachi* with the shorter weapon stuck through the wide sash-like belt round the waist of the armour. It is usually referred to as a *tantō* and translated as dagger. The difference between the two weapons is reflected in descriptions of their use, where we note the use of verbs like 'cut' and 'strike' for a *tachi* while the shorter *tantō* is employed to 'stab' and to 'thrust'. The *tachi* would be seen during a two-handed stand-off between rivals; the *tantō* would be observed when they were engaged in hand-to-hand combat, seizing each other and trying to find a weak point in the opponent's armour. There was also a whole technique around using a sword from a horse's back, although sword fighting from a horse was never easy because the normally two-handed *tachi* had to be used in one hand; however, this disadvantage was somewhat overcome by the samurai's position above a foot soldier and the momentum of his horse. The curvature of the sword's blade allowed the very hard and very sharp cutting edge to slice into an opponent along a small area that would open up to cut through to the bone as the momentum of the swing continued.

If neither archery nor *tachi* produced a direct hit or a mortal wound, the two competing samurai would try to grapple with one another using the techniques later given the name *yoroi-gumi* (armour grappling), at which point the shorter *tantō* was the favoured weapon. Pole arms were almost unknown for mounted samurai during the Gempei War although there are accounts of *naginata* being used during foot combat. Presumably an attendant would hand the weapon to his master when appropriate. *Naginata* were also the traditional weapon of the warrior monks, who are often depicted on contemporary scrolls with these weapons. The monk armies were dressed and armed identically to the samurai, with only their shaved heads or white monks' cowls showing their affiliation. The monks are always recorded as fighting very bravely but tend to be overcome in the end by the better-equipped and more ruthless samurai armies.

ARMY ORGANISATION, STRATEGY AND TACTICS

The organisation of an army during the Gempei War was far from elaborate either strategically or tactically, and in addition to their accounts of noble individual deeds the *gunkimono* often reveal how unheroic much of samurai warfare could be. Many battles were carried out by surprise attacks. These could involve a nasty business of night raids on buildings, setting them on fire and indiscriminately slaughtering all who ran out – men, women and children alike. In such cases, the ends were regarded as justifying the means. Several of the battles described here have an element of surprise built in, and there were no doubt very good military reasons for such an approach. The two armies were likely to be similarly equipped, and to catch an opponent off guard could be the only way of achieving superiority. Such episodes imply a huge discrepancy between ideal and reality in samurai warfare, but it is important to note that these two different sorts of description actually occur side by side in the same stories, with no implication that one is less moral than the other.

The only way in which samurai could ever be regarded as fighting in two different and contradictory ways lies in the very real conflict between individual glory and the need for an overall victory. Individual samurai

In spite of all the emphasis in *Heike Monogatari* on individual heroics and single combat, many of the battles of the Gempei War were won by setting fire to a building and then attacking the defenders as they ran out.

The proof that a samurai had done his duty in battle was the presentation of his enemy's severed head to the commander. Here one more such trophy is collected at the battle of Yashima in 1185.

reputations were enhanced only by personal prowess, and nowhere is this better demonstrated than in the constant obsession to win the supreme accolade of being the first into battle. Sometimes the victor of a pre-battle set-piece single combat claimed that honour, but more usually it involved being the first to enter a fortress or engage with the enemy lines, and on some occasions there was even a race between rivals to do so. For all the other samurai who were not the first into battle there was still the glory to be obtained by killing a worthy opponent, and the way that a kill was proved was through the gruesome ritual of taking the enemy's head and presenting it to one's commander. Taking a distinguished prisoner did not bestow the same accolade. Unlike in Medieval Europe, ransom was unknown.

The descriptions of the battles which follow are meant to strike the correct balance between the strategic and tactical aspects of the overall engagement and the very real nature of each encounter as a series of individual contests. A general's strategic skills in choosing ground and the logistics of supply and recruitment were all important to his success. But once battle had been joined the fight became widespread, with a multitude of opportunistic individual or group combats taking place. In these situations the samurai tended to fight their own battles with little reference to their commander. The general, for his part, would not remain sitting at the rear controlling troops and surrounded by a huge bodyguard as his descendants were to do. He would be in the thick of the fighting himself seeking out a worthy opponent.

Samurai warfare of the Gempei War does not therefore give the impression of being carried out by disciplined and drilled armies, although some discipline and organisation did exist at a micro level. This was to be found in units smaller than the overall army and consisted of groups of 20 or so warriors who supported each other, linked by family or other ties. Such a group would have been able to coordinate its movements among the overall chaos of a samurai battle. While one of their number fought his worthy opponent, the others provided support. Of the 'glue' which held these groups together family ties were the strongest, followed by long-standing lord/vassal relationships. An example of the latter would be a debt of honour to a warrior who had saved another's life. Weaker social ties were caused by the recruitment of peasant warriors, virtually by press gang, who were often poorly equipped and so carelessly registered that any

Great determination is shown on the face of this samurai as he engages a rival in single combat. His helmet is ornamented with deer antlers.

desertion was untraceable. The Taira army that pursued Minamoto Yoshinaka in 1183 lost much of its strength from peasant desertion before it came in sight of the enemy.

Battlefield control was helped by a simple system of heraldry. The particular type of flags used at this time were called *hata jirushi* and consisted of long streamers which hung from a narrow horizontal cross piece on the end of a tall pole. The *hata jirushi* were carried into battle by foot soldiers or by mounted men who rode alongside the elite samurai mounted archers. The one aspect of heraldic display at the time that is not seriously disputed is the use of red flags by the Taira and white flags by the Minamoto. As for the designs of the *mon* (badges) attributed to the two families, there is a very long tradition that associates the Taira with the *mon* of a stylised black butterfly and the Minamoto with a design based on the *rindo* (gentian) plant. Unfortunately there is no unequivocal proof for the actual use of these two *mon* during the 12th century, but every painted screen and woodblock print

This print shows Minamoto Yorinobu (987–1047) but is included here because of its depiction of the white *hata-jirushi* flag of the Minamoto ornamented by the gentian *mon* (badge) carried by a standard bearer.

depicting the Gempei War invariably shows them on the red or white flags. In the temple on the site of the battle of Yashima there is displayed a banner said to have been used by the Minamoto during the battle. It is plain white and appears to have had no emblem added to it.

There is, however, considerable circumstantial evidence that some form of device, either the actual Taira and Minamoto *mon* or other designs, did appear on their flags on many occasions. In *Heike Monogatari* there is a description of the panic caused in Kyoto when an army with white banners is seen approaching. The citizens are afraid that Yoshinaka is coming to pillage them again, but the Minamoto samurai are soon identified as Yoshitsune's men because their 'insignia are different', and calm is restored. The *maku* were another feature of the samurai battlefield where *mon* might appear. They were large cloth curtains suspended from ropes slung between poles to provide a private area for the commander and his closest retinue. Another place where motifs might be seen was on the front of the large wooden shields which the foot soldiers used for protection on the battlefield.

THE CAMPAIGN

THE GEMPEI WAR PHASE ONE: 1180–82

Minamoto Yorimasa and the first battle of Uji

Prince Mochihito's call to arms of 1180 listed the many alleged misdeeds of the Taira and promised reward to any supporters, but the proclamation referred to much more than justice and personal gain. Previous rebellions against the Taira had foundered partly on the perceived disloyalty of the insurgents towards the imperial throne. Prince Mochihito, twice passed over for the succession in favour of his Taira half-relatives, was confident that his legitimacy would overcome any hesitation the Minamoto had about supporting him, and he made this clear in the wording of his statement. One great problem that Prince Mochihito faced was that most of his potential supporters were many miles away in eastern Japan, but he had one follower who was located within the imperial court itself. This was the elderly Minamoto Yorimasa, so in spite of all its later emphasis on youthful heroics the Gempei War would begin with a warrior who was in his seventies. As a Minamoto family member, Yorimasa had suffered many insults from the Taira courtiers. He had borne the slights well and may have thought little about any notions of Minamoto revenge until the stimulus for revolutionary action came about as a result of the second snub against Prince Mochihito's succession. Yorimasa took the prince's part and urged him to rebel.

The *Kannondō* of the temple of Miidera beside Lake Biwa in Ōtsu. Miidera was one of the most important bases for warrior monks, and men from Miidera took part in the first battle of Uji in 1180.

The call to arms was also conveyed secretly to Minamoto Yoritomo in Izu province. Young Yoritomo was the great hope of the Minamoto, but he was in exile and geographically remote from the capital, and before he had time to move into action, Mochihito's plot was disclosed. Acting as efficiently as ever, Taira Kiyomori ordered that Prince Mochihito should be arrested and banished. Minamoto Yorimasa was not at first suspected of having any hand in the plot; in fact his own son was given the task of escorting Prince

The uprising by Minamoto Yorimasa and the first battle of Uji, 1180.

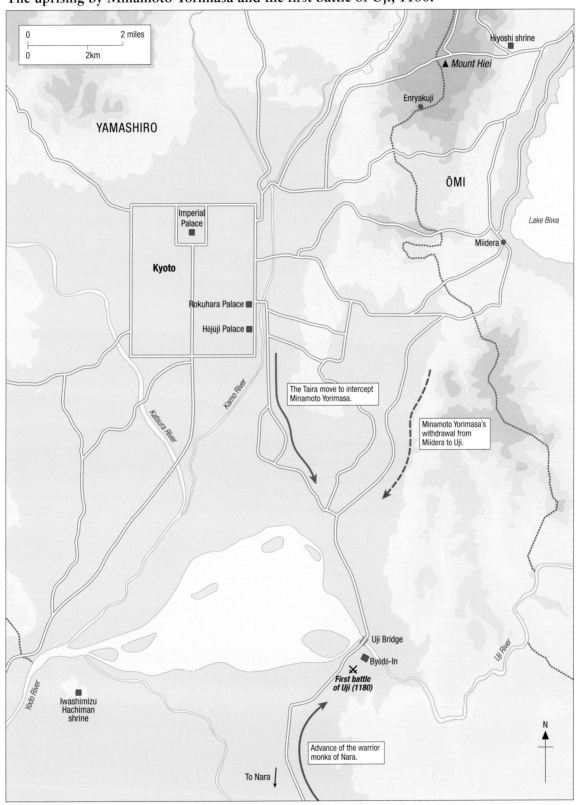

0 ___ 2 miles
0 ___ 2km

YAMASHIRO

Hiyoshi shrine

▲ *Mount Hiei*

Enryakuji

ŌMI

Lake Biwa

Imperial Palace

Kyoto

Miidera

Rokuhara Palace ■

Hōjūji Palace ■

Katsura River

Kamo River

The Taira move to intercept Minamoto Yorimasa.

Minamoto Yorimasa's withdrawal from Miidera to Uji.

Uji Bridge

■ Byōdō-In

⚔
First battle of Uji (1180)

Uji River

Yodo River

■ Iwashimizu Hachiman shrine

Advance of the warrior monks of Nara.

To Nara ↓

N
↑

Mochihito into exile on Shikoku, but Yorimasa realised that they would soon be found out. There was no time to wait for a Minamoto uprising in eastern Japan, and nearer to hand there were some anti-Taira forces which could be mobilised very quickly. These were the private armies of the Buddhist temples. Among the charges laid against Kiyomori was his contempt for existing Buddhist institutions, so Yorimasa decided to place his trust in the jealousy and resentment of the warrior monks. Together with his sons Nakatsuna and Kanetsuna he hastily fled from Kyoto and sought refuge in the monastery of Miidera on Lake Biwa. The Miidera monks began fortifying their temple by building palisades round it and adding a moat and rampart.

There Yorimasa joined Prince Mochihito, but the Taira moved swiftly to nip the development in the bud. Minamoto Yorimasa suggested a night attack on the Taira headquarters of Rokuhara in Kyoto, but this was turned down by the hesitant prince. The Taira were therefore given a free hand to advance upon the temple. Realising that Miidera would not be able to hold off a direct attack long enough for a general Minamoto rising to gain momentum, the prince and Yorimasa decided to move south and join up with the warrior monks of the Kōfukuji in Nara who had also pledged support for the anti-Taira cause. But they had to move quickly. Miidera lay to the east of Kyoto and Nara was to the south, so there was a very real danger that the advancing Taira could cut them off before they came within sight of Nara or their allies. The main strategic point along the way was the bridge over the *Ujigawa* (Uji River) at the town of Uji. The Uji River provided a very real barrier on its way from Lake Biwa to the sea and acted effectively as an outer moat to Kyoto should the capital be threatened from the south. In their flight to Nara the Minamoto used it as a moat in reverse and put the Uji River between them and their Taira pursuers. The Byōdō-In, a beautiful temple on the southern bank that had once been a nobleman's villa, became their base. In order to defend their position the Minamoto tore up the planking of the Uji Bridge and waited for whichever group would arrive first: the monk reinforcements from Nara, or their Taira enemies.

Minamoto Yorimasa may have had no more than 50 samurai under his command at the battle of Uji. The rest of his army were the monks of Miidera,

As a natural barrier between Kyoto and the south, the Uji River became the site of two battles during the Gempei War. Both involved fighting for control of the Uji Bridge, of which the present-day version is shown in the distance, and both also involved a bold crossing of the river on horseback.

and facing them was a formidable Taira army under the command of Taira Tomomori, Taira Shigehira and Taira Tadanori. The Taira vanguard arrived on the northern bank of the Uji River as dawn was breaking, although little could be seen of them because there was a thick mist over the river. Their presence was announced by the shouting of war cries and then some brave Taira samurai eager for the great honour of being first into battle galloped on to the broken bridge. Some may have perished by falling through the gap, so their advance changed into an archery duel across the river. There were also some classic instances of single combat by samurai and warrior monks balancing on the beams of the broken bridge. The *Heike Monogatari* takes great delight in relating the details of these encounters:

> Then Gochin no Tajima, throwing away the sheath of his long *naginata*, strode forth alone on to the bridge, whereupon the Heike straightaway shot at him fast and furious. Tajima, not at all perturbed, ducking to avoid the higher ones and leaping up over those that flew low, cut through those that flew straight with his whirring *naginata*, so that even the enemy looked on in admiration. Thus it was that he was dubbed 'Tajima the arrow-cutter'.

The Byōdō-In, which has miraculously survived to this day, was an aristocrat's villa until being turned into a temple in 1032. In 1180 it became the base for the defence of the Uji River by Minamoto Yorimasa and Prince Mochihito. This is its Phoenix Hall.

In this dramatic print Minamoto Yorimasa on the right gives orders to his samurai while their warrior-monk allies fight single combats on the Uji Bridge.

WARRIOR MONKS FROM MIIDERA ENGAGE THE TAIRA ACROSS THE BROKEN BRIDGE AT THE FIRST BATTLE OF UJI, 1180 (PP. 32–33)

It is early morning and the mist across the Uji River **(1)** is just lifting. On the northern bank the Taira army has gathered but are unable to cross the bridge because the defending Minamoto on the southern bank have removed a section of the planking. Nevertheless, some Taira samurai **(2)** have climbed out on to the bridge to loose arrows at the Minamoto samurai **(3)** and their allies from the warrior monks of Miidera **(4)**. That has provoked a response, and after sending arrows back three warrior monks vie with each other to be the first to clamber across the beams of the bridge and engage in honourable single combat. One is about to spin his *naginata* to deflect an arrow coming towards him **(5)**. Another deals a deadly blow to a Taira samurai, who will fall into the river below **(6)**.

We may assume that the whirling of the *naginata* was designed to put the Taira archers off their concentration rather than represent any serious attempt actually to deflect arrows. We may also reasonably assume that by the time Tajima mounted the bridge to perform his strange feat, he had exhausted his own supply of arrows because he was followed onto the broken structure by his comrade Tsutsui Jōmyō Meishū, who ran through the whole repertoire of samurai weaponry before retiring wounded:

> And loosing off his twenty-four arrows like lightning flashes he slew twelve of the Heike soldiers and wounded eleven more. One arrow yet remained in his quiver, but flinging away his bow, he stripped off his quiver and threw that after it, cast off his foot gear, and springing barefoot on to the beams of the bridge, he strode across ... With his *naginata* he mows down five of the enemy, but with the sixth the halberd snaps asunder in the midst and flinging it away he draws his *tachi*, and wielding it in the zig-zag style, the interlacing, cross, reverse dragonfly, waterwheel and eight sides at once styles of fencing, and cutting down eight men; but as he brought down the ninth with an exceeding mighty blow on the helmet the blade snapped at the hilt and fell splash into the water beneath. Then seizing the dagger which was his only weapon left he plied it as one in the death fury.

The monk Ichirai Hōshi, desperate to get into battle and standing just behind Jōmyō, seized hold of his helmet neckpiece and vaulted over him on to the beams of the bridge. Hōshi was killed, and the exhausted Jōmyō withdrew to count 63 arrows or arrow wounds in his armour or his body.

These heroics, of course, bought time for the Minamoto to be reinforced because the Taira were held on the northern bank for much of the day, but there was still no sign of any support arriving from Nara. Frustrated by the natural barrier of the Uji River, the younger and more impetuous among the Taira urged their leaders that they should attempt to ford it. Among them was Ashikaga Tadatsuna, who told his comrades how he had once taken horses across a defended river. He explained to the others how it could be done successfully and launched himself into the water. *Heike Monogatari* has him proclaiming his pedigree and achievements as he emerges on the opposite bank. We are not told if any Minamoto responded to his challenge, but the other Taira samurai certainly responded to his example and headed across the river en masse.

The ferocity of this unexpected tactic forced the Minamoto back to the gates of the Byōdō-In. Yorimasa was wounded in the elbow, and announced his intention to die by his own hand, but a group of Taira samurai threw themselves in his way. His younger son Kanetsuna engaged them to let his father escape, but while doing so an arrow struck him beneath the helmet. After a fierce session of *yoroi-gumi* Kanetsuna was overpowered and killed. His elder brother Nakatsuna was also heavily wounded, but managed to reach the Byōdō-In, where he committed suicide.

The stage was now set for the most celebrated act of battlefield suicide in samurai history. Yorimasa's *seppuku* (belly cutting, otherwise known as *harakiri*) was certainly not the first incident of its kind in Japanese history, nor was it even the first time it was performed in the heat of battle because his son had gone the same way only a few minutes earlier. Its significance lies in the details of how it was performed, and of all the precedents set by warriors in the Gempei War this one act of departure would stand alone as setting a particular standard of samurai conduct. Yorimasa first asked a loyal retainer to cut off his head. The distressed man refused, pleading as justification the lifelong loyalty he had shown to his master, but agreed to do it after Yorimasa had committed suicide. That set the first precedent. So Yorimasa turned towards the west, which was the location of paradise in Buddhist belief, and intoned ten times the *nembutsu*, the invocation of Buddha's mercy. He then completed his preparations in grand style by composing a farewell poem that read: 'Like a fossil tree from which we gather no flowers/Sad has been my life, no fruit to produce'. *Heike Monogatari* notes that composing poems at the point of death was not the usual practice but that as Yorimasa was a noted poet it was very appropriate. Nevertheless, his example would be copied many times in future battles. With that he took his dagger and sliced open his abdomen. As promised, the loyal retainer took off his head, which was weighed down with stones and thrown into the river so that it did not become a trophy for the victors.

One of the reasons for Yorimasa's heroic last stand was to allow Prince Mochihito to escape to Nara, now that they knew that the rebellion was over. He did indeed manage to fight his way out of the Uji battlefield but only got as far as a nearby shrine where, in front of its gateway, he was felled by a Taira arrow and killed. At about that moment the soldier monks of Nara arrived on the scene and, appreciating what had happened, prudently withdrew. The Nara monasteries therefore avoided the battle and escaped retribution for the time being, but it was not long before the Taira wreaked revenge against Miidera. The monks mounted a defence behind their temporary barricades and held Taira Tomomori and Tadanori at bay until nightfall, at which point the decision was taken to set fire to the temple. 'It seemed as if the Five Pleasures of Heaven had departed from the world and the Three Hot Torments of the Dragon were at their height', laments *Heike Monogatari*. Thus ended the first uprising of the Gempei War.

The grave of Minamoto Yorimasa at the Byōdō-In of Uji. Here Yorimasa performed the classic instance of *seppuku* that was to set the standard for samurai for centuries to come. He composed a farewell poem, and at the moment of incision a loyal follower took off his head.

Minamoto Yoritomo's uprising and the battle of Ishibashiyama

The opening campaign of the Gempei War had therefore finished in complete disaster. Prince Mochihito and Minamoto Yorimasa, both now dead, had made several errors of judgement. They had first of all naively assumed that possession of or traditional loyalty to the name of Minamoto would have been instantly converted into a united uprising. This had not happened in their immediate vicinity, forcing them to rely only on the warrior monks. They also failed to take into account the time that would have been needed for an uprising in the east to have an effect in the west. Instead, while the battle of Uji was being fought, the Minamoto in the east were still undecided about what to do, and all their attention had fallen on the young exile Yoritomo.

By 1180 Yoritomo was recognised by friend and foe alike as the leader of the scattered and diverse Minamoto, and the social connections provided by his father-in-law allowed him to become widely known and respected particularly within the key eastern provinces of Sagami and Suruga that bordered Izu. As well as receiving Prince Mochihito's proclamation Yoritomo must also have speedily learned of the latter's death, but instead of abandoning the rebellion as a lost cause he began rallying Minamoto supporters to his banner. This proved to be a formidable task. A contemporary genealogy lists 161 families in the north and east of Japan as being of Taira descent compared to 136 with Minamoto ancestry, so Yoritomo would have been highly dependent on samurai from other families who had pledged allegiance to the Minamoto at some time in their careers. Other factors were that 20 years had gone by since the Minamoto were last in action and Yoritomo was an untried force. The samurai who agreed to follow Yoritomo in his initial operation were therefore a mixed bunch that included men who were nominally Taira even though they had all once served Yoritomo's late father Yoshitomo. Of important local lords only the Chiba and the Miura had sent representatives to Yoritomo, and they were not around when the fighting began.

Matters came rapidly to a head on 13 July 1180 when news arrived that Taira Kiyomori had ordered Yoritomo's capture and execution. The command to act had been given to Taira Kanetaka, the deputy governor of Izu, so Yoritomo planned a pre-emptive strike against Kanetaka's headquarters of Yamagi. The raid was planned for dawn on 8 September. Yoritomo's force was pitifully small. He depended heavily on the Sasaki family of Sagami, one of only two families of Minamoto descent that had responded to Yoritomo, but they reported late for the muster and almost caused Yoritomo to postpone his assault to 9 September. If so it would have taken place on the day of the Buddhist ceremony for the liberation of all sentient beings from confinement, which worried the devoutly religious Yoritomo. Instead the operation against Yamagi was changed to a night attack on the 8th rather than a dawn raid on the same day. *Azuma Kagami* relates a typical incident of samurai warfare on the way towards Kanetaka's headquarters, when the brothers Sasaki Takatsuna and Sadatsuna approached the residence of a Taira supporter called Tsutsumi Nobutō:

> Then Takatsuna moved up to the edge of the courtyard and released an arrow.
> This was the moment of the beginning of the Minamoto war against the Taira.
> A bright moon above made the night as bright as midday. Nobutō's followers,
> seeing Takatsuna's challenge, shot their arrows at him, while Nobutō, his long
> sword in hand, went forth round toward the south-west to confront Takatsuna.

The campaigns of Minamoto Yoritomo in the Kantō, and Ishibashiyama (1180).

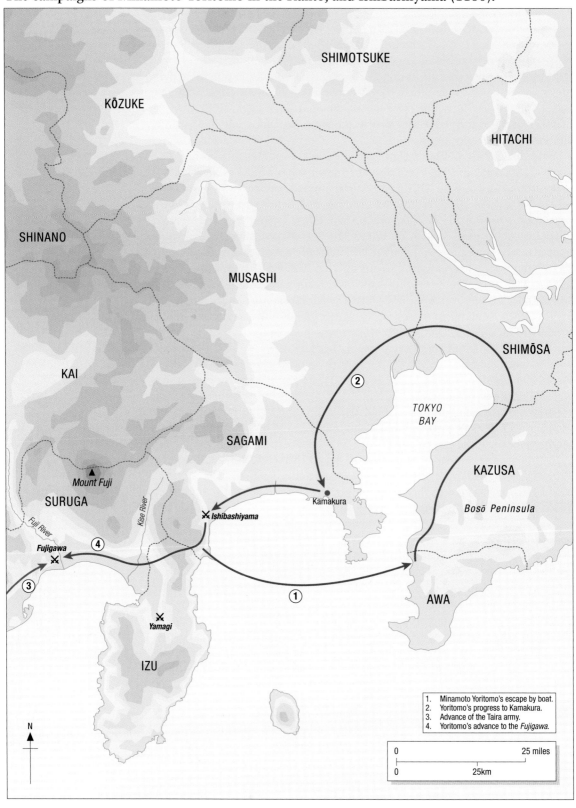

SHIMOTSUKE

KŌZUKE

HITACHI

SHINANO

MUSASHI

SHIMŌSA

TOKYO BAY

KAI

SAGAMI

KAZUSA

Bosō Peninsula

Mount Fuji

SURUGA

Kamakura

Fuji River

Kise River

② Ishibashiyama

Fujigawa

④

③

①

AWA

Yamagi

IZU

N

1. Minamoto Yoritomo's escape by boat.
2. Yoritomo's progress to Kamakura.
3. Advance of the Taira army.
4. Yoritomo's advance to the *Fujigawa*.

0	25 miles
0	25km

The latter discarded his bow, grasped his long sword, and facing his adversary to the north-east, engaged him in combat. Both excelled in bravery, but Takatsuna was struck by an arrow. At that moment Sadatsuna came up from the rear and slew Nobutō.

The bright moon continued to illuminate the scene for the subsequent night attack on Yamagi, where Taira Kanetaka was killed. Yoritomo therefore won his first encounter with the Taira, although he did not take part personally. Instead he stayed at his headquarters and prayed for victory, after which he enjoyed his first experience of head-viewing after a battle.

With the leading Taira sympathiser in the area overcome, Yoritomo could consider leaving Izu province for Sagami to raise support among other Minamoto sympathisers, but there was a formidable foe there in the person of Ōba Kagechika. Although he was a hereditary vassal of the Minamoto, Kagechika firmly supported the Taira and had just returned from Kyoto where he had helped to restore order in the capital after the first battle of Uji. Fearing that Yoritomo would soon be reinforced by local families such as the Miura after his success at Yamagi, Kagechika felt that he could not delay his move against the young upstart. Kyoto was too far away for him to receive detailed orders from Taira Kiyomori, so Ōba Kagechika took full charge of the operation. Among the men led by Kagechika in what became the battle of Ishibashiyama we note Kumagai Naozane (who one day would fight for the Minamoto) and Itō Sukechika, whose daughter Yoritomo had once seduced.

This modern print shows Minamoto Yoritomo in action at the battle of Ishibashiyama in 1180. His defeat in a narrow mountain valley was the only occasion on which the future Shogun took a personal role in combat. His return to power afterwards was a remarkable turn around in Minamoto fortunes.

Ishibashiyama is a narrow valley that leads inwards from the sea on the Izu Peninsula a short distance to the south of modern Odawara. Ōba Kagechika had 3,000 men with him and made armed contact with Yoritomo, who commanded one-tenth of that number, on 14 September, only six days after Yoritomo's successful attack on Yamagi. The rough terrain did not favour mounted fighting so the battle was largely a dismounted affair where swords would have been as important as bows. The night saw cold weather with driving rain and strong winds, in the midst of which the Taira launched their two-pronged attack. While the forces under Ōba Kagechika held the Minamoto in place, Itō Sukechika advanced secretly from Izu to fall upon Yoritomo's rear. Yoritomo's men 'cherished their friendship for their leader and all fought with a determination to die, if necessary, for Yoritomo,' says *Azuma Kagami*. They did indeed fight desperately all night, but with the dawn they were forced to flee while Kagechika's men, 'loosening arrows and hurling rocks', gave chase. In marked contrast to his absence from the scene at Yamagi, Minamoto Yoritomo could not avoid taking a full part in the fighting at Ishibashiyama and acquitted himself well. *Azuma Kagami* tells us that his 'arrows found their aim with unerring accuracy'.

Yoritomo escaped with great difficulty from his defeat at Ishibashiyama and endured a series of narrow escapes in the depths of the Hakone Mountains that were highly romanticised in subsequent accounts. One celebrated story has him hiding in a hollow tree. Kajiwara Kagetoki, a secret Minamoto sympathiser, was given the task of investigating the tree and managed to disturb some wood pigeons, thereby saving Yoritomo's life. Yoritomo then worked his way round towards the coast and took a ship over to the safety of the province of Awa at the tip of the Bosō Peninsula on the far side of what is now known as Tokyo Bay. He was then given the depressing news that the pro-Minamoto army under Miura Yoshiaki, who had failed to join Yoritomo at Ishibashiyama, had themselves been defeated. It looked as though the Minamoto uprising was over as soon as it had begun.

The Taira response and the battle of the Fujigawa

The defeated Minamoto Yoritomo landed on the coast of Awa on 19 September 1180. On 26 October he made a triumphal entry into the traditional Minamoto 'capital' of Kamakura, a place not far from his point of departure, after a month that had seen the most remarkable reversal of fortune in Japanese history. Yoritomo's journey, a major turning point in the Gempei War, involved making an anti-clockwise sweep through the provinces of Awa, Kazusa, Shimōsa, Musashi and Sagami in an almost complete circle. The trip today would take a visitor through much of urban Tokyo, Kawasaki and Yokohama. Yoritomo made his way through rich farming land, much of which had owners with a traditional sympathy for the Minamoto. In that month, therefore, Yoritomo raised an army while running away. He had been met on his arrival in Awa by Miura Yoshizumi and was also joined there by his father-in-law Hōjō Tokimasa. With them he began a campaign to win the hearts and minds of any hesitant supporters along the way. The late Prince Mochihito may have given imperial legitimacy to the cause, but it is likely that opposition to the local deputies appointed by the Taira had more effect on the decision-making processes of these tough and independent eastern warrior lords.

In Kazusa province Chiba Tsunetane threw in his lot with Yoritomo. In Musashi province Edo Shigenaga also pledged himself to the Minamoto cause, and distant news came to Yoritomo's ears that his cousin Kiso Yoshinaka, also exiled as a child, had risen in rebellion among the mountains of Shinano province. Several minor lords also joined him, so that by the time he entered Kamakura, Minamoto Yoritomo was at the head of a large and confident army. *Azuma Kagami* puts it at 200,000 strong, which is an impossibly large figure, but the extent of Yoritomo's influence is hard to dispute. His headquarters of Kamakura was then little more than a fishing village, but because of a long family connection with the Minamoto it was the natural base for him, and to make the point Yoritomo was able to take up residence in his late father's mansion. Yet not all his allies submitted willingly; the reluctant Satake family would have to be pacified into supporting the Minamoto cause.

The news of Yoritomo's uprising was reported as quickly as possible to Taira Kiyomori, but soon after there came the announcement of the Taira victory at Ishibashiyama, so for a while they could breathe again. In fact, with two separate Minamoto rebellions safely crushed the Taira felt confident about taking the fight to the east. On 20 October, while Yoritomo was still making his sweep through the Kantō, an army was assembled to destroy him once and for all. It should have set out in great spirits, but the prevailing feeling was one of dread. There were rumours that Prince Mochihito had escaped unharmed from Uji and that it was he who was fomenting the continued disturbances. But the most important factor was the looming threat of a famine. It would come to its worst point in 1182 when hostilities would cease, but there was already evidence that a food shortage was imminent. It was not a good time for a major expedition.

Yoritomo kept himself very well informed about the Taira progress and prudently sent his uncle Minamoto Yukiie to make contact with Minamoto supporters in Kai province, whose position to the north of the Taira's line of march along the *Tōkaidō*, the great eastern sea road, made them ideal for interrupting their progress. Kai, marked by the presence of Mount Fuji, bordered Suruga, which was drained to its east and west respectively by the *Kisegawa* (Kise River) and the *Fujigawa* (Fuji River). On 2 November Yoritomo was told that the Taira army had entered Suruga. Leaving Kamakura he joined Takeda Nobuyoshi, leader of the Kai Minamoto supporters. By now the Taira had reached the *Fujigawa*, and Minamoto made plans to give battle to them somewhere in Suruga. Events ensured that the matter was resolved much earlier than Yoritomo had planned.

It is certain that the morale of the Taira army, which was under the command of Taira Koremori, was very low. Supplies had been even more difficult to obtain than they had anticipated, and now the Taira samurai were about to encounter a Minamoto army on its home ground. The *Fujigawa* was not a moat like the *Ujigawa* had been. It was wide and meandering and could be crossed with care, but it provided an ideal place to rest and regroup the Taira forces with the river between them and their enemies. By now the Minamoto had reached its eastern bank and set up camp themselves, and it would appear that Takeda Nobuyoshi, probably on his own initiative, decided to make a reconnaissance in force. His army crossed some distance away from the rival camps, and even though they were only 600 strong, Nobuyoshi decided that a night raid on the Taira would be a useful conclusion to their expedition. They may have raised their war cry as they attacked, but the mere presence of the Takeda soldiers was enough to disturb a huge flock of waterfowl, probably some form of geese, which flew towards the Taira lines with a deafening shriek of their voices and beating of their wings. This caused confusion and panic among the Taira, and hearing the commotion the bulk of Yoritomo's army began to cross the river in support of their comrades. The result was a massacre of those they caught in the Taira camp, but there could be no immediate pursuit in the darkness. Yoritomo withdrew his victorious troops across the river and thus provided a short breathing space for the Taira to organise what was to become a fairly well organised retreat back to Kyoto. Although usually presented as a tragi-comical event that hardly deserves the title of 'the battle of the *Fujigawa*', the encounter was a real armed confrontation. It was also the first head-on meeting between the two rivals and gave Yoritomo a genuine and much-needed early victory to assure his new supporters that their trust was not misplaced. Taira Tadakiyo is credited with organising the Taira's successful retreat, which contradicts *Azuma Kagami*'s claim that the Taira samurai threw away their armour, jumped on to the nearest horses available and that only ten samurai made it back to the capital. The withdrawal was certainly rapid and took nine days, and on 19 November the demoralised samurai under the disgraced Koremori re-entered Kyoto and faced the wrath of Kiyomori. So bitter was the experience of the *Fujigawa* that a Taira army would never pass that point again during the entire Gempei War.

Minamoto Yoritomo wanted to press on and take the imperial capital himself, but considerations of the support the Taira still enjoyed there and growing evidence of food shortages soon made him change his mind. It was time to consolidate his position in Kamakura, and the most important step that Yoritomo took in what would one day become the administrative capital of Japan was his founding of the *Samurai-dokoro* (Samurai Office), an institution that marks the modest beginning of the *bakufu* or Shogunate, the military dictatorship that Yoritomo's eventual triumph would impose upon Japan. Through the decrees of the *Samurai-dokoro* Yoritomo officially approved and confirmed the original rights and claims of his followers as they had been before the Taira had started meddling in their affairs. Not long after *Fujigawa* he was also reunited with his brother Yoshitsune, who had been living in exile far to the north under the guardianship of the Ōshū Fujiwara family in Hiraizumi (in modern Iwate Prefecture). The man who was to become one of Japan's greatest generals was now ready for action.

Back in Kyoto, the disheartened Taira commanders discovered that other rebellions were brewing. Kiso Yoshinaka in Shinano would soon develop into a major threat, but samurai in distant Kyūshū had also risen in revolt. In Kyūshū's Higo province the Kikuchi rebelled against the Taira deputy, while in Satsuma at Kyūshū's southern tip a man who bore the surname of Taira, Taira Tadakage, raised a rebellion that proved very successful in this remote area. He would still be making trouble for Yoritomo in 1187. Nearer to home Ōmi province, whose rice lands were traditionally Kyoto's larder, saw considerable unrest. In Kii province a loose coalition of coastal pirates and priests from the great shrines of Kumano who felt they had been slighted in favour of Itsukushima were causing trouble. On 9 December Taira Tomomori took the fight to the rebels of Ōmi and defeated Yamamoto Yoshitsune who was in league with the warrior monks of the Kōfukuji in Nara. This was no dignified field battle with noble challenges, because 'Tomomori and his vast forces set fire to the Yamamoto manor house and the houses of the Yamamoto followers, thus causing consternation in the Genji ranks and forcing them to flee', says *Azuma Kagami*.

This involvement by the monks of Nara was significant and proved very costly to them, because on 15 January 1181 Taira Shigehira and Taira Michimori took a dreadful revenge. The monks fortified their temples with palisades and ditches and held off the Taira attack, which *Heike Monogatari* notes was made by mounted samurai against monk soldiers fighting on foot. The resistance was desperate, so Shigehira ordered the use of fire against the defences using chopped-up wooden shields. He may well have intended it to be a limited operation but the flames quickly spread to the buildings of the Kōfukuji and on to the national treasure of the Tōdaiji, with its colossal wooden main temple hall containing the Daibutsu, the world's biggest bronze statue of Buddha. The temple was destroyed along with hundreds of people who had sought sanctuary in it and, 'the colossal statue of Vairochana Buddha of copper and gold, whose domed head towered up into the clouds, from which gleamed the scared jewel of his lofty forehead, fused with the heat, so that its full moon features fell to the pavement below, while its body melted into a shapeless mass'. Through the burning of the Nara temples Taira Kiyomori lost any remaining vestiges of support or respect from the powerful religious arm of Japanese society. Two months later, on 20 March 1181, the great statesman or tyrant, depending upon one's allegiance, died in a raging fever that was inevitably seen as divine punishment. His last words were a request to place upon his tomb the head of Minamoto Yoritomo.

An encounter between the warrior monks of Nara and the Taira samurai is the subject of this highly detailed painted scroll. On the extreme left a cowled monk with a *naginata* takes on a similarly armed samurai. The mounted combat involves far more than conventional archery. One is even using a *kumade* (rake) to pull his opponent from the saddle. In the foreground a foot soldier suffers a head wound.

The revolts noted above were now spreading so widely that a response had to be made, and in fact the Taira then won one of their few victories. It was gained at the expense of Minamoto Yukiie, the uncle of Yoritomo, at Sunomata on the border of Owari and Mino on 25 April. It is an interesting encounter because the battle involved one side crossing a river and the other responding in kind. In *Heike Monogatari*, 'The Genji force crossed over and made a sudden assault with the intention of taking the Heike by surprise, but the latter quite undismayed, allowed them to penetrate deeply with the small force, and then closed in and surrounded them, and as they were all dripping with water after fording the river this served to distinguish friend and foe'. Then the Taira under Tomomori and Shigehira crossed the river themselves and landed on Minamoto-occupied shore to take 600 heads, but they lacked the resources to follow up their victory.

As 1181 progressed, the Taira turned their attentions towards Kiso Yoshinaka, who was busily carving out a territory for himself in Shinano and Echizen provinces, largely unaware of the famine that was beginning to grip the Taira heartlands and the political consolidation that was proceeding apace in Kamakura. The food situation was now so serious that Yoritomo actually proposed a truce with the Taira. The peace offer was rejected, and because they lacked the resources to tackle Yoritomo directly, a Taira ally in Echigo province took the initiative and raised an army to attack Kiso Yoshinaka's base in Shinano. The raid was unsuccessful and the combined forces of Kiso Yoshinaka and the Takeda counter-attacked at the battle of Yokotagawara on 27 July. Kiso disguised some of his troops as Taira warriors and crushed the invaders:

> The Genji of Shinano, by the stratagem of Inoue no kuro Mitsumori, divided two thousand of their men into seven parties, each bearing a red flag, the colour of the Heike, and when the warriors of Echigo saw these emerging over the rocks and out of the defiles they set up a shout of joy, thinking that many were for their side in this province also. But as the different bands approached, at a given signal the whole seven drew together into one, and throwing away their red banners, suddenly replaced them with white ones and advanced to the onset. When the men of Echigo saw this manoeuvre panic seized them and they cried out: 'Ah! We have been deceived!'

Yokotagawara was a setback for the Taira, but towards the end of 1181 they managed to quell the rebels in distant Kyūshū, which provided some comfort. When 1182 began, Japan finally buckled under the Great Famine, and for almost an entire year the Gempei War was suspended.

THE GEMPEI WAR PHASE TWO: 1183–84

Kiso Yoshinaka and the battle of Kurikara

Hostilities recommenced at the beginning of the year 1183 when the focus of the Gempei War shifted to a different part of Japan and to two very different personalities. Of the leaders who had so far controlled military matters from a distance, one, Taira Kiyomori, was now dead and his place at the head of the Taira clan had been taken by his less than capable son Munemori. The Taira's leading opponent Minamoto Yoritomo was still very much alive, but

The campaigns of Kiso Yoshinaka in the Hokurikudō, and Kurikara (1183).

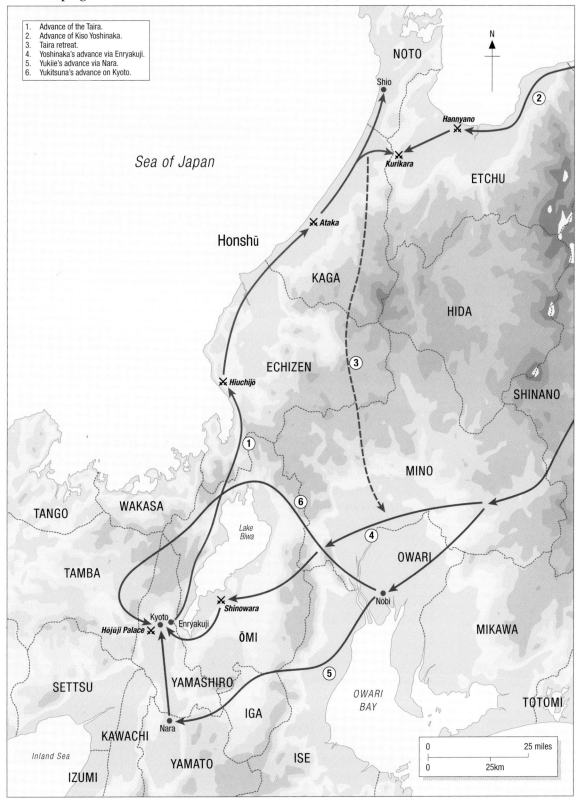

1. Advance of the Taira.
2. Advance of Kiso Yoshinaka.
3. Taira retreat.
4. Yoshinaka's advance via Enryakuji.
5. Yukiie's advance via Nara.
6. Yukitsuna's advance on Kyoto.

the veteran of Ishibashiyama and *Fujigawa* would no longer be seen on any battlefield. From now on others would do the fighting for him and the final victory would be delivered by his brother Minamoto Yoshitsune, yet as far as the year 1183 was concerned the Minamoto general whose name begins to dominate the narrative is Yoritomo's cousin, the reckless and impulsive Kiso Yoshinaka.

The Taira considered that Yoshinaka was a greater threat than Yoritomo, and for the time being they were right because Yoshinaka was rapidly building up his strength in the *Hokurikudō*, the area along the Sea of Japan coast that stretched from the southern part of Dewa province through Echigo, Etchū, Kaga and Echizen and on into Wakasa, a province uncomfortably close to Kyoto. In distant Kamakura Yoritomo monitored these developments and recalled the old Chinese adage that there cannot be two suns in heaven. He was the leader of the Minamoto, not Yoshinaka. It is strange to read of Yoritomo opposing the man who was about to defeat the Taira on the Minamoto's behalf, but the situation reflects the true nature of the Gempei War as a complex struggle.

The death of Kiyomori had changed the Taira's political situation as well. The accession of the weak Taira Munemori had allowed Cloistered Emperor Go-Shirakawa to assert himself once again in the imperial court, so while Yoshinaka was busy with his military preparations Yoritomo secretly contacted this important power behind the throne to suggest some form of accommodation. Go-Shirakawa, he felt, would be a crucial ally against both the Taira and Yoshinaka. The latter was probably unaware of these developments, but he fully appreciated his cousin's hostility towards him and tried to reassure Yoritomo by sending his son Yoshikata to Kamakura as a hostage to guarantee his good intentions.

By the spring of 1183 Taira Munemori felt sufficiently confident to ignore Go-Shirakawa and mount a military expedition against Yoshinaka, even though it would involve a march into the *Hokurikudō* at a time when the country was only just recovering from famine. The sheer scale of the operation also indicated that the debacle at the *Fujigawa* had taught them nothing, because the Taira only managed to assemble a large army by using recruiting methods that were little more than press-ganging farmers into becoming soldiers. 'We carry neither bows nor swords,' was the complaint recorded in one quarter by a man taken unwillingly from his fields.

The notional strength of the Taira expeditionary army was 100,000 men, and at the end of April they began to march under the command of Taira Koremori in a northern direction into Echizen to confront Yoshinaka. On 20 May they came upon a Minamoto outpost at Hiuchijō, a simple stockade fortress that was built on rocky crags and was well defended. The Minamoto had built a dam to create a moat, which hindered the Taira assault until a traitor fired an arrow telling them how to breach the dam and run off the water. After this the fortress soon fell to the Taira. Yoshinaka's force retreated and four days later were beaten again at Ataka on the sea coast of Kaga province. These two victories against Minamoto outposts reassured the Taira leaders, but in spite of these minor triumphs Yoshinaka's greatest victory lay just around the corner.

From this point on matters get very confusing. Somewhere in the vicinity of modern Kanazawa the Taira divided their army into two. The smaller unit, said to be 30,000 strong and under Taira Michimori, continued northwards in the direction of Shio in Noto province. Minamoto Yukiie was sent to take care of them, but no battle would be fought because the defeat at Kurikara would leave them isolated. The main body of 70,000 under Koremori followed the *Hokurikudō* as it bore east to cross from Kaga province into Etchū province (modern Ishikawa and Tonami prefectures) through the Pass of Kurikara, and it was there that Yoshinaka would defeat them in battle on 2 June 1183. There was however a mysterious curtain raiser to Kurikara, because Koremori's 5,000-strong vanguard under Taira Moritoshi apparently pressed on quite far ahead of the main body and went well into Etchū. There they were defeated by Yoshinaka's general Imai Kanehira at a place called Hannyano on 31 May. What is unclear is the path that Moritoshi's men then took, because they do not seem to have affected the outcome of the battle of Kurikara in any way.

This fine modern statue of Minamoto Kiso Yoshinaka stands on the site of his greatest victory at the pass of Kurikara in 1183.

Probably ignorant of the fate of his vanguard Taira Koremori continued on up the *Hokurikudō*, much of which still exists in its original form as a footpath that intersects the modern road at various intervals, and the overall topography of mountains and valleys is also relatively unchanged. The Taira climbed steadily, passing the peak of Jōgamine (195m) and shortly afterwards levelling out through the Pass of Kurikara, of which the highest point is marked by a Buddhist temple called the Fudōji at a height of 277m above sea level. The pass then continues downwards to the east beneath Tonamiyama (263m), but just to the south of the Fudōji is a fairly extensive area of flat ground called Sarugababa, and there the Taira stopped. It was a decision forced on them by Kiso Yoshinaka, who was currently based at the foot of the pass on its eastern side. Yoshinaka wanted them to stay at the top of the Pass of Kurikara. To achieve this he detached 3,000 men under Yoda Jirō from his total army of about 40,000 and sent them up the pass on 1 June with a number of white banners that was far in excess of what would be expected for a small force. They took up their decoy positions just to the north of the road on a hill. This served to discourage the Taira from continuing any further down the pass when what appeared to be a huge army lay to their left flank. They therefore set up a fortified camp at Sarugababa to await attack on ground of their own choosing, aligned towards Yoda's force.

All this was perfectly in accord with Yoshinaka's plans because to the south-east the flat ground of Sarugababa dropped away very steeply into a valley now called *Jigokudani* or 'Hell Valley'. It would be so named after the 'hell' the Taira encountered there during the battle, because Yoshinaka's intention was to force the Taira down into this enclosed death trap that divided Sarugababa from another hill now called Gempeigamine. There they would be caught by three units of his army who were stationed overlooking the dead end of Hell Valley. They were under the command of Imai Kanehira (6,000), Nenei Yukichika (4,000) and 3,000 under one other, whom a persistent tradition identifies as Tomoe Gozen, Yoshinaka's famous warrior wife, whose career will be discussed later. There was certainly a third unit present, but no name for their commander is given in *Heike Monogatari*. The Taira would be driven down into Hell Valley by a surprise flank attack under Higuchi Kanemitsu, who was now heading up the pass behind the Taira army with 4,000 men. To keep its move secret, that unit had been forced to carry out a long and time-consuming sweep round to the north and then follow the Taira up the pass, so to buy the time necessary for the rear attack to materialise Yoshinaka planned to use his remaining main body of about 20,000 men in a holding action by setting in motion the traditional requirements of the classic battle. He therefore headed up by a route somewhat to the north of the pass and drew up his lines to the left of Yoda Jirō's decoy troops. Not knowing that they were slowly being surrounded, at dawn on 2 June the Taira army joined in enthusiastically in a very rare example of a samurai battle conducted in the way that everyone believed that they should be fought. There was first a succession of archery exchanges performed by groups of 15, 50 and then 100 mounted samurai, no doubt with the most noble challenges being uttered and accepted. After this the two groups fought each other hand to hand as a proxy for the total armies.

Yoshinaka was careful not to let the fight develop into an all-out melee. Instead he carefully restricted the Minamoto involvement until night began to fall. This gave time for his other contingents to prepare, and as the sun set, Yoshinaka's encircling force rushed along the *Hokurikudō* up the pass from the west to attack the Taira on their left flank. As the Taira reacted to this surprise, they met a further shock to their right. Curiously, this incident does not appear in *Heike Monogatari*, but a very strong tradition maintains that Yoshinaka's men had rounded up a herd of at least 100 head of oxen and tied torches to their horns. The signal to act was the noise of the attack by the encircling force, and when the torches were fired the enraged oxen whipped

The most popular story associated with the battle of Kurikara concerns Yoshinaka's use of a herd of oxen who had burning brands attached to their horns. When the brands were lit, the herd charged off towards the Taira lines and caused panic. Strangely, the story does not appear in *Heike Monogatari*, but has been reproduced here on the battle site itself.

off along the pass towards the west. Some Taira samurai were knocked clean off the path by the frantic herd. Yoshinaka's main body then launched a full attack from the front. There was nowhere for the Taira to escape along the road either to east or west, so they were driven backwards down into Hell Valley, which had no easy exit. Yoshinaka's detached units then rode down into the valley and massacred them. *Heike Monogatari* notes: 'Thus did some 70,000 horsemen of the Taira perish, buried in this one deep valley; the mountain streams ran

with their blood and the mound of their corpses was like a small hill.' A pursuit continued as the survivors tried to make their way to safety.

There seem to have been a number of running battles after Kurikara. The route of the Taira flight and Yoshinaka's pursuit was straight to the south through Kaga and Echizen, but Yoshinaka then turned off into Owari because he is reported as having joined up with his uncle Minamoto Yukiie at Nōbi sometime in July. Yoshinaka then headed straight for Kyoto, defeating Taira Koremori, who had retreated following Kurikara, at the battle of Shinowara in Ōmi. The battle began with an archery duel between ten champions from each side, after which the fight became a general one. Several celebrated single combats took place there, and a good example of archery followed by classic swordplay is found in the *Heike Monogatari* account:

> Arikuni, having penetrated very deeply into the ranks of the foe, had his horse shot from under him, and then while he was fighting on foot, his helmet was struck from his head, so that he looked like a youth fighting with his long hair streaming in all directions. By this time his arrows were exhausted, so he drew his sword and laid about him mightily, until, pierced by seven or eight shafts, he met his death still on his feet and glaring at his enemies.

Another account shows the use of the short sword for a swift opportunistic stroke against a samurai opponent:

> Takahashi got off his horse to recover his breath and waited to see if any of his retainers would come up, and Nyūzen also dismounted, but, still thinking what a feat it would be to kill such a famous leader, even though he had just spared his life, he cast about to see how he could take him unawares. Takahashi, never dreaming of such treachery, was talking to him quite without reserve, when Nyūzen, who was famous for the rapidity of his movements, catching him off guard, suddenly drew his sword and aimed a lightning thrust under his helmet.

There was one poignant moment during the battle of Shinowara because among the casualties was a samurai whose face looked familiar when his head was brought for inspection by Yoshinaka. His hair was black, but when the head was washed, he was revealed as the white-haired old warrior Saitō Sanemori, then aged 72, who had dyed his hair to appear younger. Many years before Sanemori had been ordered to kill the child Yoshinaka, but had instead become instrumental in helping him escape to the mountains of Shinano. At Shinowara Sanemori fought to the last against Yoshinaka, who was greatly moved when his identity was revealed.

At the battle of Shinowara in 1183 a head was brought for inspection to the victorious Kiso Yoshinaka. He had the head washed and the black hair dye disappeared to reveal the white-haired Saitō Sanemori, a veteran samurai who had once saved Yoshinaka's life.

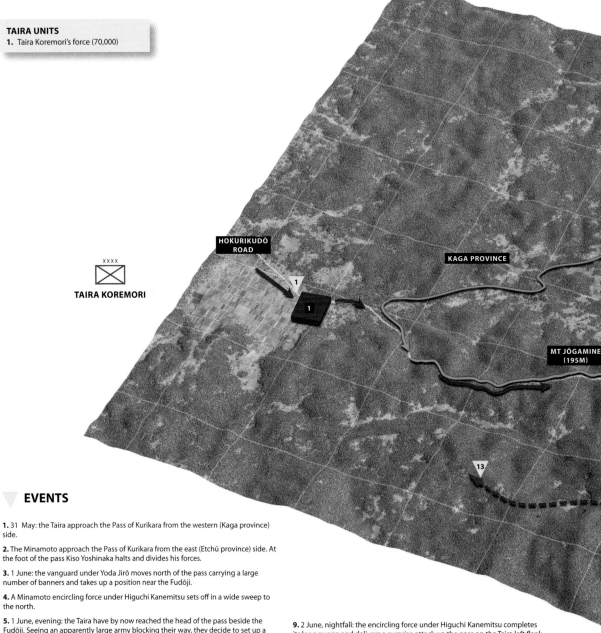

TAIRA UNITS
1. Taira Koremori's force (70,000)

HOKURIKUDŌ ROAD

KAGA PROVINCE

XXXX

TAIRA KOREMORI

MT JŌGAMINE (195M)

▼ EVENTS

1. 31 May: the Taira approach the Pass of Kurikara from the western (Kaga province) side.

2. The Minamoto approach the Pass of Kurikara from the east (Etchū province) side. At the foot of the pass Kiso Yoshinaka halts and divides his forces.

3. 1 June: the vanguard under Yoda Jirō moves north of the pass carrying a large number of banners and takes up a position near the Fudōji.

4. A Minamoto encircling force under Higuchi Kanemitsu sets off in a wide sweep to the north.

5. 1 June, evening: the Taira have by now reached the head of the pass beside the Fudōji. Seeing an apparently large army blocking their way, they decide to set up a fortified camp at Sarugababa.

6. Imai Kanehira, Nenei Yukichika and Tomoe Gozen make their way to the south to take up positions surrounding *Jigokudani* (Hell Valley).

7. Moving just to the north of the pass, Yoshinaka's main body joins Yoda to take up a position opposite the Taira.

8. 2 June, dawn: Yoshinaka's main body engages the Taira in a holding action between the lines until nightfall.

9. 2 June, nightfall: the encircling force under Higuchi Kanemitsu completes its long sweep and delivers a surprise attack up the pass on the Taira left flank.

10. As this happens, a herd of oxen with flaming brands is released along the pass from the east.

11. Yoshinaka's main body launches a full attack from the north.

12. The Taira are driven down into Hell Valley where the three detached units attack them.

13. The Taira survivors flee into Kaga with the Minamoto in hot pursuit.

THE BATTLE OF KURIKARA, 2 JUNE 1183

Yoshinaka's forces trapped the Taira forces in the Pass of Kurikara, leaving them no route of escape along the road either to east or west. The Taira forces were driven backwards down into Hell Valley, where Yoshinaka's detached units massacred them. *Heike Monogatari* notes: 'Some 70,000 horsemen of the Taira [perished], buried in this one deep valley; the mountain streams ran with their blood and the mound of their corpses was like a small hill.'

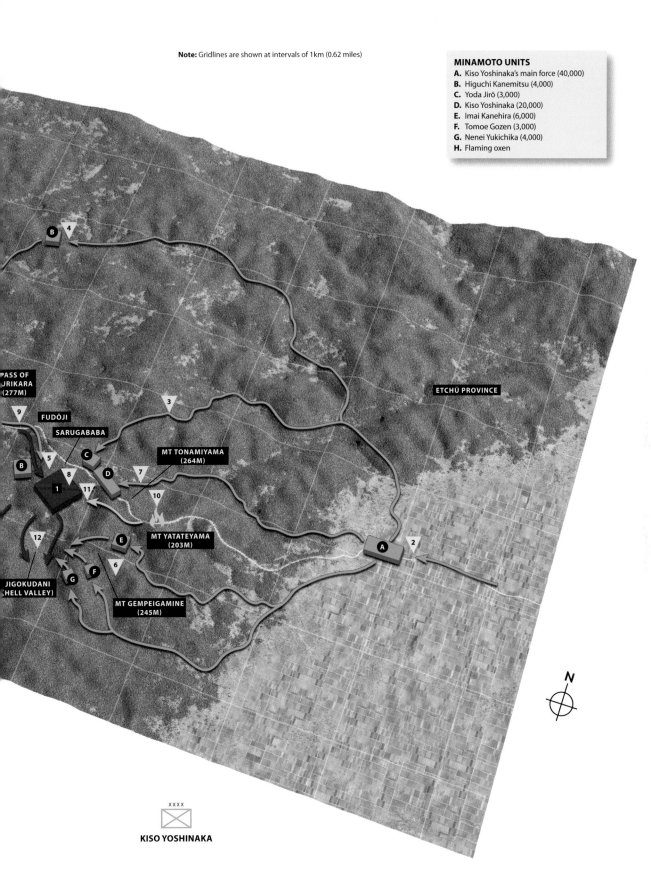

Note: Gridlines are shown at intervals of 1km (0.62 miles)

MINAMOTO UNITS
A. Kiso Yoshinaka's main force (40,000)
B. Higuchi Kanemitsu (4,000)
C. Yoda Jirō (3,000)
D. Kiso Yoshinaka (20,000)
E. Imai Kanehira (6,000)
F. Tomoe Gozen (3,000)
G. Nenei Yukichika (4,000)
H. Flaming oxen

PASS OF
URIKARA
(277M)

ETCHŪ PROVINCE

FUDŌJI

SARUGABABA

MT TONAMIYAMA
(264M)

MT YATATEYAMA
(203M)

JIGOKUDANI
(HELL VALLEY)

MT GEMPEIGAMINE
(245M)

N

XXXX
KISO YOSHINAKA

The spectacle of the survivors of Kurikara and Shinowara straggling into Kyoto greatly alarmed the population of the capital. With the Taira crushed in two engagements nothing could now prevent Yoshinaka from entering Kyoto as victor, but he planned his advance very carefully as a three-pronged approach to catch the Taira in a trap. One contingent under the little-known Minamoto Yukitsuna circled round Kyoto to the north to attack from the west. Yoshinaka himself took the direct route along the *Tōkaidō* beside Lake Biwa, while Yukiie went through Ise and Iga provinces to approach Kyoto from the south via Uji. Yoshinaka, however, did not rush into Kyoto. Following his reunion with Yukiie he had opened up negotiations with the warrior monks of Enryaku-ji on Mount Hiei. They had been spared the destruction inflicted upon Nara and their daughter temple of Miidera, so on 11 August Yoshinaka entered Enryaku-ji, from whose mountainous location all of the city of Kyoto could be seen in the plain below. Kyoto was his for the taking, and while still on Mount Hiei he received an unexpected and illustrious visitor when Go-Shirakawa came secretly to meet him and hailed him publicly as the conqueror of the Taira.

The endorsement by Go-Shirakawa was an enormous boost for Yoshinaka and a tragedy for the Taira. Feeling totally abandoned and knowing that he was nearly surrounded, Taira Munemori took action, which was not to attack Yoshinaka but to flee from Kyoto along with the boy emperor Antoku, the bulk of the imperial family and the vital crown jewels, the possession of which confirmed an emperor's legitimacy. The three items of the imperial regalia – the mirror, the sword and the jewel – are the objects that were, and still are, the symbols that guarantee the eternity of the imperial throne and have always played an important role in Japanese history. Relying on the Taira's control of the Inland Sea, Taira Munemori headed for a place of safety. Several bases linked by efficient sea-crossings afforded protection and the first lay due west from Kyoto at Fukuhara in present-day Kōbe city, which was defended by the fortress of Ichinotani. Across the Inland Sea on Shikoku was Yashima (now the city of Takamatsu), while at the most westerly point of the Inland Sea in Nagato province (modern Shimonoseki city) lay the territory of Taira Tomomori and the island of Hikojima. The ongoing rebellions on Kyūshū noted above meant that the Taira would not dare go any further than Nagato, but that would be safe enough from the landlubbers in the Minamoto clan. The bases could be linked and reinforced by boat, but it meant that from this moment on until the end of the Gempei War the imperial family and their Taira protectors became shipboard nomads, shuttled from one safe port to another.

Go-Shirakawa and the battle of the Hōjūji Palace
On 17 August 1183, three days after the imperial escape, Yoshinaka and Yukiie entered Kyoto at the head of three armies. In the description in *Heike Monogatari* Yoshinaka rapidly changes from being a victorious general to acting as a crude and cruel boor. His rough mountain warriors behave as if the city had been given over to them for pillage by robbing, raping and killing anyone regardless of age, sex or political affiliation to Taira or Minamoto. Neither Yoshinaka nor Yukiie did anything to stop them, and their own ignorant behaviour in Court soon convinced Go-Shirakawa that he had made a colossal error of judgement in hailing Yoshinaka as a liberator. He had even given Yoshinaka the prestigious title of *asahi shōgun* (the general of

the morning sun). The Taira may have been Go-Shirakawa's greatest enemies, but he now appreciated that the true leadership of his Minamoto allies lay not with Yoshinaka's mob rule but with Yoritomo in Kamakura. So Go-Shirakawa wrote to Yoritomo inviting him to come and liberate the capital from his cousin. The result was that Yoshinaka's control of Kyoto would last less than six months.

Unfortunately, because of the grip exerted by his marauding samurai, Kiso Yoshinaka was in firm charge of Kyoto and had ideas of his own. His first move was to dismiss any pro-Taira courtiers he could find; his second was to insist on the appointment of a new emperor. Emperor Antoku had slipped away with the Taira so a replacement was needed, and one was found in the person of the younger brother of the former emperor Takakura. The latter, who had been forced to abdicate in favour of Emperor Antoku, had since died, so under Yoshinaka's orders his brother, another child emperor, became Emperor Go-Toba. Because of the absence of the crown jewels Go-Toba could not be properly installed, but Yoshinaka was satisfied that the

After the battle of Kurikara the samurai of Kiso Yoshinaka, shown here on this print, pillaged Kyoto and lost whatever goodwill they had acquired by crushing the Taira army.

Minamoto cause he represented now had genuine imperial legitimacy. Yoshinaka also felt confident enough to mount a new expedition against the Taira in pursuit of the regalia, so he and Yukiie gathered their armies and headed west. Yoshinaka went along the Inland Sea coast while Yukiie proceeded further inland through Tamba province.

The result of Yoshinaka's advance along the *San'yōdō*, the Honshū coast road of the Inland Sea, was the first naval encounter between the Taira and the Minamoto. It ended with a Minamoto defeat. Unlike the long marches that had led to their defeats at Fujigawa and Kurikara, the Taira were now on home ground and exploited their naval strength at the battle of Mizushima on 17 November 1183. Mizushima was the name of an island on the Inland Sea in Bitchū province, and from there, according to *Heike Monogatari*, Yoshinaka was planning to sail over to Shikoku to attack the Taira base of Yashima. A Taira fleet under Tomomori and Noritsune came and intercepted him. An unusual naval battle then developed, because the Taira ships were made fast alongside each other by hawsers tied from stern to stern, and between these hawsers other ropes were fastened on which planks were stretched for walking across, so that the whole fleet became a level surface for the fighting men. The description of the fighting therefore sounds more like a land battle involving an exchange of arrows and single combat with the only difference being the fact that both grapplers and wounded fell into the sea. For example, one of the Minamoto samurai, Yada Yoshikiyo, 'sprang into a small boat with six of his retainers, and led a fierce attack in the very forefront of the battle, but all in vain, for his boat was capsized by the enemy and all in it were drowned'. The Taira had their horses with them on their boats and as they approached the shore, the horses were made to swim to land. The Taira samurai then waded ashore and mounted up, at which Yoshinaka's men stationed on land were scattered. It was a useful victory for the Taira, and it boded well for the future. They had been right to place their trust in their naval strength and the local factor of loyal support that was also involved was confirmed when they heard that Minamoto Yukiie had been defeated. In his case the battle was fought on the same day as Mizushima at a place called Muroyama in Harima province.

It was around 1 December 1183 that the shocked and defeated armies of Yoshinaka and Yukiie re-entered Kyoto. By then Yoshinaka must have known about Go-Shirakawa's contact with Yoritomo because the latter had circulated the news widely, so it was as an angry man that he confronted the ungrateful ex-emperor, whom he, Yoshinaka, had liberated from the Taira yoke. Go-Shirakawa knew that he was under threat so, seeking protection from Yoshinaka and playing for time until Yoritomo's army arrived from the east, he began fortifying his Kyoto residence. This was the Hōjūji Palace, which was located just to the east of the famous Sanjūsangendō temple between *Shichijō* (7th Street) and *Hachijō* (8th Street) according to Kyoto's ancient grid pattern. The place incorporated a temple called the Hōjūji and the present site houses Go-Shirakawa's tomb. On 1 January 1184 it was attacked by Yoshinaka in a little-known action, and although the battle may be insignificant compared to what was shortly to follow, it represents Kiso Yoshinaka's last victory and also encapsulates the tactics, techniques and traditions of the Gempei War in microcosm. The description in *Heike Monogatari* also provides a rare reminder of the realities of samurai warfare.

Yoshinaka divided his men into seven separate attacking units. As a sign of recognition they all wore a badge of pine leaves. Yoshinaka led the advance against the palace's main gate, where he was confronted by a bold and defiant samurai who reminded Yoshinaka that it was unthinkable to draw weapons against an imperial personage. So strident were the man's protestations that everyone thought he had been possessed by a *tengu*, but Yoshinaka was nonplussed. 'At the same time Higuchi no Jirō and his two thousand men rushed into the attack with loud shouts from the direction of Imakumano, and Imai himself, putting fire to the head of a turnip-headed arrow, shot it so that it stuck in the roof of the Hōjūji Palace, and as the wind was blowing strongly, the flames immediately shot up into the air'. The defenders raced away from the flames, tripping over their bows, dropping swords and *naginata* so that the blades cut their legs as they ran. When they reached the end of *Shichijō*, they came under an unusual form of attack because Go-Shirakawa's men had taken up positions on the rooftops to catch Yoshinaka's troops as they fled, and began throwing stones down upon their own comrades by mistake. The presence of these missiles is simply explained by the Japanese practice of weighing down roof shingles using lines of stones, so that, 'Many were killed, and others with their heads or backs crushed, fell from their horses and managed to crawl away to some place of refuge.' The extreme end of *Hachijō* was held by warrior monks and Imai Kanehira loosed an arrow at one (who was presumably not wearing a helmet) that pierced clean through his skull so that he fell backwards from his horse.

Meanwhile Go-Shirakawa was also attempting to escape from his burning palace, but so great was the confusion that some of his own samurai loosed arrows at his palanquin. The non-combatant Taira Yorisuke, the governor of Bungo province, was also in the Hōjūji Palace when the fight started. When he fled from the flames, he too was attacked by a band of samurai and stripped naked, and 'the cold wind from the river cut him to the bone'. Greater concern was felt for the child emperor Go-Toba, so he was put in a boat and launched on the ornamental lake of the palace to avoid the flames, but some samurai fired arrows at him too. Go-Shirakawa eventually made it to safety in another Kyoto palace, but, as *Heike Monogatari* puts it in a profound understatement, 'the Imperial Procession was of a pitiably attenuated kind'. There then occurred an unusual example of a samurai issuing a challenge to single combat when a battle is winding down:

> 'I am Jirō Kurando Nakayori of Shinano, 27 years old, the second son of Shinano no kami Nakashige and a descendant in the ninth generation of Atsuzane Shinno. Come, anyone who think himself somebody and let us see!' And he swung his sword about him, cutting and slashing in all directions, until at last he fell, borne down by the weight of numbers.

With this final flourish the battle ended, and the following day Yoshinaka took part in a head-viewing ceremony. There were 630 brought before him. After this his men gave their war cry and Yoshinaka's final victory was complete. He could hardly have suspected that he had only two months left to live.

Yoshitsune's advance and the second battle of Uji

Following the battle of the Hōjūji Palace, Yoshinaka undergoes his second and final transformation in *Heike Monogatari* from being a cruel oppressor to dying as a tragic hero. The narrative now begins to express sympathy for him, and it starts with the approach of his cousins Minamoto Noriyori and Minamoto Yoshitsune, who were under orders to destroy him. At the end of February 1184 Noriyori entered Ōmi province and was heading for the Seta Bridge at the tip of Lake Biwa, but Yoshinaka was worried most about Yoshitsune, who was approaching from the south and would have to cross the Uji Bridge. Yoshinaka decided to use the river as a defence in reverse from the situation in 1180. Staying behind in Kyoto from where he could reinforce either army, he sent Nenei Yukichika and Tate Chiketada to defend the approaches. They destroyed the Seta Bridge but left the Uji Bridge alone, presumably so that it could be used to mount a counter-attack. To defend the river they placed stakes in its bottom at the known crossing points and tied ropes between them.

The second battle of Uji therefore began. Yoshitsune's samurai, who had no doubt heard of the famous exploits from 1180, hoped to emulate those examples themselves and on 3 March 1184 a race began to become the first across the river. This contest to be the first into battle was fought between Sasaki Takatsuna and Kajiwara Kagesue. Their rivalry was to become one of the best-known episodes of the Gempei War and has often been reproduced in art. Takatsuna was one of the four Sasaki brothers who had almost arrived too late for Yoritomo's raid on Yamagi in 1180, while Kajiwara Kagesue was the son of Kajiwara Kagetoki, the man who had saved Yoritomo's life by disturbing two wood pigeons. As they rode down towards the river, Kagesue took an early lead, until Takatsuna called out a warning that his saddle girth was loose. This would have been a very dangerous situation for a horseman swimming his mount across a river, so the grateful Kagesue dismounted to tighten it, only to find that he had been tricked. Sasaki Takatsuna was now well ahead and in the river. Using his *tachi* from the saddle he cut through the ropes that Yoshinaka's men had tied between the stakes and rode on to the opposite bank and samurai glory. Kajiwara Kagesue was not far behind him, but the current carried him downstream. Hundreds of samurai followed them.

Kajiwara Kagesue, the loser of the race across the river at the second battle of Uji in 1184, is shown here in this modern painted scroll.

The defence of the bridge was therefore nullified and resistance soon collapsed. Word was hastily taken to Yoshinaka, who prepared to leave Kyoto to fight. Meanwhile Minamoto Yoshitsune hurried northwards towards Kyoto to make his presence known to Go-Shirakawa. When the

This print is an interesting depiction of the race across the Uji River in 1184. Both samurai are shown as swimming in very deep water, holding on to their horses. Note the pillars of the Uji Bridge and the arrows flying above their heads.

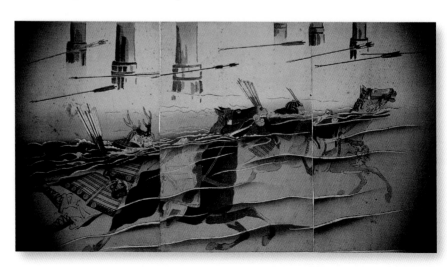

The second battle of Uji, and the battle of Awazu (1184).

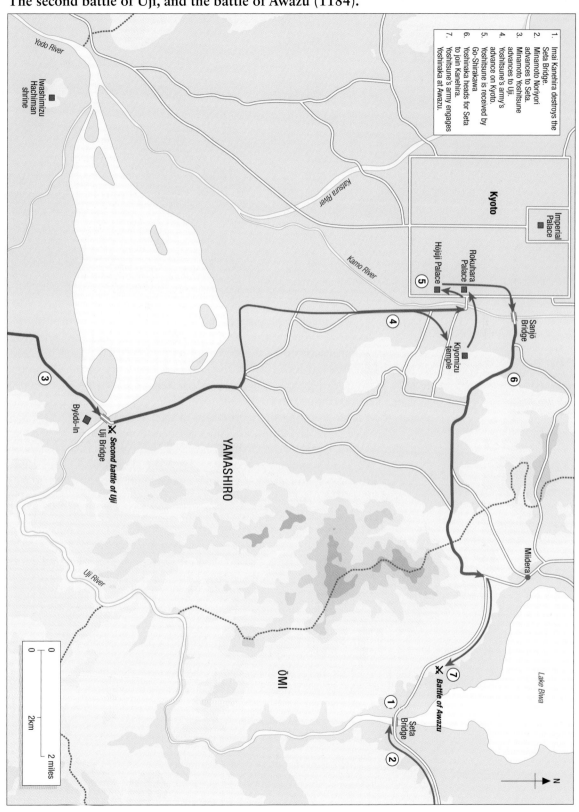

1. Imai Kanehira destroys the Seta Bridge.
2. Minamoto Noriyori advances to Seta.
3. Minamoto Yoshitsune advances to Uji.
4. Yoshitsune's army's advance on Kyoto.
5. Yoshitsune is received by Go-Shirakawa.
6. Yoshinaka heads for Seta to join Kanehira.
7. Yoshitsune's army engages Yoshinaka at Awazu.

Following the example set by Sasaki Takatsuna and Kajiwara Kagesue, hundreds of Minamoto samurai rode into the Uji River while their comrades fought across the damaged bridge.

citizens first saw the white banners of the Minamoto on the streets of Kyoto, they were terrified, thinking that Yoshinaka's rapacious mob had returned. They were soon reassured by the different insignia they saw upon the flags as Yoshitsune entered Kyoto from the east in the vicinity of the Kiyomizu temple. Yoshinaka's precise whereabouts are not clear, but he was now in danger of being trapped in Kyoto so made the decision to head east in the direction of Ōtsu and the ruins of the Seta Bridge. That was where his most loyal follower Imai Kanehira, the man who had performed so well at Kurikara and the battle of the Hōjūji Palace, was fighting against Minamoto Noriyori, who had somehow managed to cross the Uji River at Seta. As the entire area to the east and south of Kyoto was swarming with hostile samurai, it looked as though Yoshinaka had decided to die an honourable death.

Tomoe Gozen and the battle of Awazu
When Yoshinaka made contact with Imai Kanehira, he is said to have had at his side his wife, the female samurai warrior Tomoe Gozen. Her name was mentioned earlier because of a tradition linking her to the battle of Kurikara. The account of Tomoe Gozen fighting at the battle of Awazu in *Heike Monogatari* is so brief that it can easily be recounted in full as follows:

> Tomoe had long black hair and a fair complexion, and her face was very lovely; moreover she was a fearless rider, whom neither the fiercest horse nor the roughest ground could dismay, and so dexterously did she handle sword and bow that she was a match for a thousand warriors, and fit to meet either god or devil. Many times she had taken the field, armed at all points, and won matchless renown in encounters with the bravest captains, and so in this last fight, when all the others had been slain or fled, among the last seven there rode Tomoe.

After describing Yoshinaka's final manoeuvres the account returns to Tomoe Gozen:

But now they were reduced to but five survivors, and among these Tomoe still held her place. Calling her to him Kiso said, 'As you are a woman, it were better that you now make your escape. I have made up my mind to die, either by the hand of the enemy or by mine own, and how would Yoshinaka be shamed if in his last fight he died with a woman?' Even at these strong words, however, Tomoe would not forsake him, but still feeling full of fight she replies, 'Ah, for some bold warrior to match with, that Kiso might see how fine a death I can die!' And she drew aside her horse and waited. Presently Onda no Hachirō Moroshige of Musashi, a strong and valiant samurai, came riding up with 30 followers, and Tomoe, immediately dashing into them, flung herself upon Onda and grappling with him, dragged him from his horse, pressed him calmly against the pommel of her saddle and cut off his head. Then stripping off her armour she fled away to the eastern provinces.

Tomoe Gozen is Japan's most famous samurai woman warrior. (Photograph kindly supplied by Lella and Gianni Morra, Fine Japanese Prints, Illustrated Books and Works of Art, Venice, Italy)

That is the last we hear of her in *Heike Monogatari*, although other *gunkimono* add that Yoshinaka expressly directed her to take the story of his final battle back to their home province of Shinano. Before leaving the field she was attacked by Wada Yoshimori, one of Yoritomo's chief retainers, using a pine trunk as a club. She twisted the trunk in her hands and broke it into

Tomoe Gozen takes the head of the enemy samurai Onda Moroshige by grappling with him and holding him against her saddle.

THE DEATH OF KISO YOSHINAKA AT THE BATTLE OF AWAZU IN 1184 (PP. 60–61)

Kiso Yoshinaka **(1)** has captured Kyoto from the Taira, but this has won him few friends. Now his cousins have broken through his defences at Uji and Seta, forcing Yoshinaka to flee from the imperial capital. He chooses not to escape but to join his comrade Imai Kanehira, who is fighting off Minamoto samurai near Seta. At Awazu and in the midst of sporadic and confused fighting Kiso's horse **(2)** crashes through the ice on a deep paddy field. As Yoshinaka tries to free himself, an enemy archer **(3)** spots him and rides up to deliver a close-range shot. The arrow strikes Yoshinaka in the forehead, killing him instantly.

splinters, but Wada Yoshimori caught her and made her his concubine. She was to bear him a son, the celebrated strong man Asahina Saburō Yoshihide who was killed in 1213 when the Wada family were destroyed by the Hōjō. Tomoe then became a nun and lived to the age of 91. With that Japan's greatest female samurai warrior would pass out of history, but back at Awazu the stage was set for one of the finest accounts of a samurai's last moments. In *Heike Monogatari* we read:

> Yoshinaka rode off alone to Awazu, and it was the 23rd day of the first month. It was now nearly dark and all the land was coated with thin ice, so that none could distinguish the deep rice fields, and he had not gone far before his horse plunged heavily into the muddy ooze beneath. Right up the neck it foundered, and though Kiso plied whip and spur with might and main, it was all to no purpose, for he could not stir it. Even in this plight he still thought of his retainer, and was trying to see how it fared with Imai, when Miura no Ishida Jirō Tamehisa of Sagami rode up and shot an arrow that struck him in the face under his helmet. Then as the stricken warrior fell forward in his saddle so that his crest bowed over his horse's head, two of Ishida's retainers fell on him and struck off his head.

This painted scroll of Kiso Yoshinaka hangs in the temple of Gichūji in Ōtsu, not far away from the battlefield of Awazu where he was killed by a sharpshooter's arrow.

Note that Yoshinaka's killer has to 'ride up' in order to deliver a close-range shot against the immobilised Yoshinaka and that his companions take the head on their master's behalf. With Yoshinaka gone Imai Kanehira had nothing to live for, so he committed a spectacular act of suicide. Kanehira took the point of his sword between his teeth and dived headlong from his horse on to the frozen ground so that the sword was driven clean through his skull.

Minamoto Yoshinaka's career as a samurai commander had been brief but glorious. His victory at Kurikara was a brilliant tactical masterpiece involving deception and initiative as well as more traditional samurai skills. He also clearly inspired his men and was served by a handful of devoted followers. But Yoshinaka's genius was limited to the battlefield situation. The behaviour of his troops and his own unwillingness to act the role of courtier aroused strong resentment when he entered Kyoto. Yoshinaka thereby played straight into his wily cousin's hands. Had it not been for the political genius of Yoritomo, which contrasted markedly with Yoshinaka's political naivety, Minamoto Kiso Yoshinaka could well have become the first Shogun of Japan.

THE GEMPEI WAR PHASE THREE: 1184–85

Minamoto Yoshitsune and the battle of Ichinotani

With the death of Kiso Yoshinaka the Gempei War enters its final phase where the military narrative is dominated by the generalship of Minamoto Yoshitsune, the young leader who had demonstrated his military talents at the crossing of the *Ujigawa*. Go-Shirakawa fully recognised the part Yoshitsune had played in ridding him of Yoshinaka, so he held a triumphant entry into the city for the Minamoto army. But Yoshitsune and Noriyori had not long to enjoy any rest, because within a few days they would be setting out from Kyoto in pursuit of the Taira, acting under their brother's orders and with a new imperial commission from the Cloistered Emperor.

The sole objective in the third phase of the Gempei War was the final elimination of the Taira, and it was a daunting prospect. Yoshinaka's defeat at Mizushima and Yukiie's at Muroyama had confirmed where the Taira strength really lay, and at that time the Minamoto had nothing with which to counter it. Their one hope was to catch the Taira while they were still on land and defeat them before they had a chance to escape to the sea. The first of three battles to attempt such a coup was fought at Ichinotani on the coast of Settsu province and provides some of the richest and most varied accounts of fighting in the whole of *Heike Monogatari*. The descriptions involve a surprise attack, single combat and, in an almost unique example during the Gempei War, an attack on a defended fortress.

Ichinotani is one of the best-known conflicts in the Gempei War, but it is also much misunderstood. There are no reliable accounts of the numbers involved, although they are likely to have been about 7,000 on each side. In some accounts the battle is described as being launched not against Ichinotani but the Taira base at Fukuhara, a place that has now disappeared under modern Kōbe city. Fukuhara had been Taira Kiyomori's pride and joy. He had lavished attention upon its harbour to encourage trade along the Inland Sea, and following the Taira victory at Uji in 1180 palaces and mansions were built there. For six months it became the imperial capital of Japan with the Emperor Takakura in residence until the courtiers complained of the distance from Kyoto and the wet

His victory over Yoshinaka at Uji confirmed Minamoto Yoshitsune's position as the military leader of the Minamoto. Here he is beside Lake Biwa, with the hill on which Miidera is built behind him.

weather. It is likely that some of the former imperial residences were still in existence in 1184, but most of the action during the battle took place not within Fukuhara itself (of which the probable location has been identified by modern archaeology) but some distance to the west at the place called Ichinotani.

The new rationale for the Taira having a base outside Kyoto was not upon maintaining a detached palace but instead on garrisoning a fortress. Ichinotani was of course not a developed Japanese castle like 17th-century Himeji with its huge stone base and multi-storeyed keep. Instead it was a wooden stockade typical of the age that would have enclosed within it the living quarters (*shinden*) for the Taira nobles and their imperial grandson. Subsidiary buildings would be attached to the *shinden* by covered corridors. The open courtyard from which the *shinden* was secluded would contain living quarters for the samurai, stables and gates, latrines and wells, and surrounding all this would be a strong wooden palisaded wall, either of horizontal planking or rough vertical timbers. The only use of stone would have been the ones used to hold down the roof shingles as noted above for the Hōjūji battle. The key entrances to Ichinotani would be covered by fortified gatehouses, and several types are illustrated in contemporary scrolls. They would be built from heavy timbers, and above the gates, which swung open on iron hinges, would be guard rooms. A parapet for archers extended all the way round the tower and access was provided by a ladder through a trap door. Modifications may have included the augmentation of the parapet wall by using the familiar large wooden shields set up on battlefields. These raised the height of the wall by a small amount. Other pictorial sources show the hanging of heavy cloths bearing the defenders' *mon* from frameworks above a gate. Both types would catch spent arrows and prevent an attacker from looking inside the fortress from any nearby elevated position.

Ichinotani lay in a naturally strong position beneath steep cliffs that were thought to be impassable. On the southern side its wooden walls opened on to the sea where the Taira had moored their ships for a fast getaway. The developed port at Fukuhara had been effectively abandoned, and in fact when the battle began Taira Munemori was already on board ship with Emperor Antoku and the crown jewels, leaving others to defend Ichinotani. The Taira expected any attack on Ichinotani to be launched along the beach from the east through Fukuhara, where Taira Tomomori provided an outer line of defence that could safely be abandoned for the security of the fort while buying time for an escape. Their assailants Yoshitsune and Noriyori had envisioned just such a strategy, so they had planned a much bolder move to catch the Taira before they had a chance to take to the sea. Minamoto Noriyori took the shorter direct approach, marching in a south-westerly direction from Kyoto and reaching the Inland Sea in the vicinity of modern Nishinomiya. From there he worked his way along the coast to launch the assault on the

The main gates of the fortress of Ichinotani probably looked very much like this reconstruction at the Fujiwara Heritage Village in Iwate Prefecture. It is made from massive timbers with an encircling parapet that slopes slightly outwards. There is a central gatehouse.

The campaigns of Yoshitsune and Noriyori against the Taira, 1184–85.

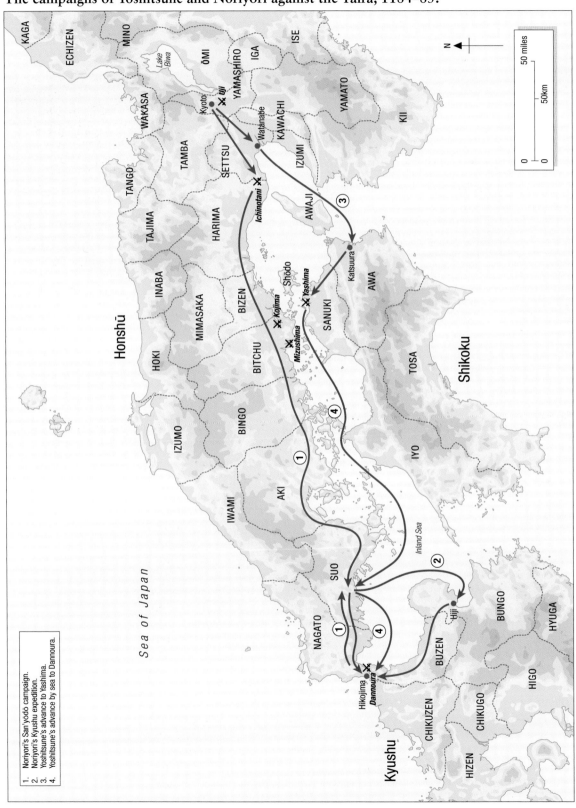

1. Noriyori's San'yōdō campaign.
2. Noriyori's Kyushu expedition.
3. Yoshitsune's advance to Yashima.
4. Yoshitsune's advance by sea to Dannoura.

defenders of Fukuhara, as the Taira had anticipated. Yoshitsune, however, made a wide detour through the mountains that border Kyoto to the north-west, passing through Tamba province and approaching Ichinotani from the north. At the last moment he divided his forces yet again, sending the bulk of his army under Doi Sanehira to approach along the beach from the west while he made the surprise rear attack for which the battle would become famous.

There was a brief prelude to the battle of Ichinotani on the night of 18 March when Yoshitsune's army overran the Taira outpost of Mikusayama. Its way was lighted by burning torches and the Minamoto took the Taira completely by surprise. It was not long after this operation that he divided his army and sent Doi Sanehira to complete the three-way assault from the west. The main attack on Ichinotani cannot have been a surprise. The raid on Mikusayama would have announced their presence from that direction and *Heike Monogatari* tells us that the battle of Ichinotani was in fact delayed for religious reasons. The day the Minamoto had planned turned out to be scheduled for Buddhist rites for the departed Taira Kiyomori, which would have made the day unlucky for anyone who disturbed the rituals, and the following two days were unlucky anyway according to beliefs derived from the calendar.

Once the auspicious day arrived, Yoshitsune reached the hills behind Ichinotani at a place called Hiyodorigoe. Although it was a cliff edge, it had a sufficient slope for a descent to be possible, but the ground was broken by rocks and vegetation and was very steep in places with patches of loose ground that would give way under the weight of men and horses. Locals believed that the way down Hiyodorigoe was so dangerous that not even a monkey could manage the descent, but that was Yoshitsune's intention. However, on the night before the battle Yoshitsune's strategy was questioned by some of his followers, not on the grounds of safety, but because the rear attack would make it less likely for those taking part to achieve the supreme accolade of being the first into battle.

Kumagai Naozane was the first to draw that conclusion, and realised that a more promising course of action would be to join Doi Sanehira's forces that were massing for the main attack along the beach. Naozane and his son Naoie therefore detached themselves from Yoshitsune's forces and went to join Doi Sanehira, but instead of linking up with their comrades their thirst for individual glory meant that they deliberately passed them by and rode straight up to the walls of Ichinotani. Naozane called out his name to the defenders, hoping for a worthy challenge. None came, and the

A view of the battlefield of Ichinotani looking down from the top of the Hiyodorigoe, the cliff side down which Yoshitsune led the surprise attack that captured the fortress.

67

THE FIGHT ON THE BEACH AT ICHINOTANI IN 1184 AND THE DEFIANCE OF KAGIWARA KAGESUE (PP. 68–69)

The Minamoto have overrun the Taira fortress of Ichinotani and various single combats are taking place up and down the beach. Kajiwara Kagesue **(1)** has become isolated from other Minamoto; his horse has been brought down and his helmet knocked off his head. With all his arrows exhausted, he has drawn his sword, his hair streaming in the wind, with arrows protruding from his armour. The exhausted Kagesue leans against a rock **(2)** as the Taira dead **(3)** begin to mount up around him. Although he is prepared for death, Kagesue's father will soon arrive, allowing him to fight his way to safety.

Kumagai pair soon realised that they were not alone because they had been joined by a fellow samurai called Hirayama Sueshige who had similar aspirations. Sueshige's challenge finally drew a response and a small unit of Taira samurai came out to fight them. The Minamoto warriors supported each other until the Taira were driven back inside Ichinotani. Naozane's horse was shot from under him. He then began to pull arrows out of his armour and drew his sword. Forced to fight on foot, Naoie joined him but he was wounded in the left forearm. The concerned Naozane urged his son to readjust his armour so that no unnecessary weak points were exposed. The two of them then took on a mounted Taira samurai and beat him off using their *tachi*. Meanwhile Hirayama Sueshige's standard bearer was killed so Sueshige forced his way into Ichinotani and took the head of the man who had felled him. An argument then began about who had been the first into battle, and *Heike Monogatari* closes the chapter with the issue unresolved.

Their example prompted other Minamoto samurai to make their own challenges as the battle developed and Doi Sanehira took on Taira Tadanori's defenders. Tadanori had been one of the victors of the first battle of Uji and was also a survivor of Kurikara. Among the Minamoto heroes was Kajiwara Kagetoki, whose son Kagesue, the hero of the Uji crossing, was wounded and disappeared from view. While searching for him Kagetoki took great delight in issuing a challenge and proclaiming his descent from a hero of a century earlier who had attacked a similar stockade in northern Japan and received an arrow in his eye. He is supposed to have pulled the arrow out unaided and used it to kill the enemy marksman. When Kagetoki finally found his son the youth presented the appearance of the classic wounded samurai, 'dismounted and fighting on foot, for his horse had been shot under him, with his helmet struck off from his head and his long hair flying in the wind, his back against a rock 20ft high and two of his retainers on his left and right, fighting desperately with five soldiers of the Heike'. When his father arrived, Kagesue fought his way out and survived.

In spite of all these valiant individual heroics, or perhaps because of the time wasted in performing them, neither of the flank attacks made any impression on the walls of Ichinotani. When Doi Sanehira pressed forward his main assault, it was valiantly resisted by Taira Tadanori. Noriyori was expected to be on his way after driving back Taira Tomomori from Fukuhara, so it was therefore up to Minamoto Yoshitsune to achieve their primary objective by a surprise rear attack. Yoshitsune first sent two riderless horses down the slope, and when they appeared at the bottom with no injuries he led his army down to fall in surprise on the defenders of Ichinotani. The going was as difficult as everyone had expected, but the surprise worked. They stormed the rear of Ichinotani, which was relatively unguarded, and set fire to every building they came across. The leaping flames cause panic among the Taira defenders, who ran for the beach and the boats that would provide their means of escape. As noted earlier, the emperor and the regalia were already out at sea so the great prize sought by Yoshitsune was already lost, but the expanse of beach provided an unusual occasion for acts of single combat to be fought after a battle was effectively over rather than before it began. These took place on the sand as the Taira tried to escape to their boats, and a good example is the single combat between Etchū Zenji Moritoshi and Inomata Noritsuna:

The dramatic descent of the Hiyodorigoe is captured perfectly here as a life-sized diorama at the Heike Monogatari Museum in Takamatsu (Kagawa Prefecture). Yoshitsune leads the charge followed by Benkei.

Rushing upon each other, they grappled fiercely so that both fell from their horses ... he gripped his adversary and pinned him down so that he could not rise. Thus prostrate beneath his foe, try how he would to shift him or draw his sword, he could not so much as stir a finger to the hilt, and even when he strove to speak, so great was the pressure that no word would come forth ... he suddenly sprang up from the ground and dealt Moritoshi a heavy blow on the breastplate with his closed fist. Losing his balance at this unexpected attack, Moritoshi fell over backwards, when Inomata immediately leapt upon him, snatched his dagger from his side, and pulling up the skirt of his armour, stabbed him so deeply thrice that the hilt and fist went in after the blade. Having thus despatched him he cut off his head.

The list of high-ranking Taira casualties at Ichinotani was quite considerable, and the first example of a senior death is the account in *Heike Monogatari* of the killing of Taira Tadanori. Okabe Tadazumi, an ambitious Minamoto samurai, spotted him and followed at full gallop, eager to take his head. When challenged, Tadanori claimed to be a Minamoto but Tadazumi noted that he had adopted the courtier's custom of blackening his teeth, so he tackled him and the fight led to a *yoroi-gumi* contest that was not all one way. He may have looked effeminate but Tadanori was very strong:

Clutching Tadazumi he pulled him from his horse, dealing him two stabs with his *tantō* while he was yet in the saddle, and following them with another as he was falling. The first two blows fell on his armour and failed to pierce it, while the third wounded him in the face but was not mortal, and as Tadanori sprang down upon him to cut off his head, Tadazumi's page, who had been riding behind him, slipped from his horse and with a blow of his sword cut off Tadanori's arm above the elbow.

Knowing that his end had come, Tadanori pushed Tadazumi away and said a quick prayer, and when he finished Tadazumi took his head. Elsewhere on the beach Taira Shigehira, the second-in-command at Ichinotani and the man who had burned Nara, was attempting to make his escape. A Minamoto samurai brought down his horse so Shigehira crawled into the water to commit suicide by *seppuku*. His pursuer did not allow this to happen and instead of removing Shigehira's head he took him prisoner, a great disgrace for a samurai.

Every individual death at Ichinotani added to Yoshitsune's victory, but out of all the single combats that took place none is better known than the tragic incident whereby Kumagai Naozane, the warrior who had already claimed to be the first into the battle, killed Taira Atsumori. Their fight is one of the most famous episodes in *Heike Monogatari* and was to spawn many plays and ghost stories. Atsumori is the archetype of the gentle, effeminate courtier samurai more fond of poetry than fighting. Naozane has him at his mercy and is inclined to spare the life of a youth of the same age as his son Naoie. Naozane had been moved when Naoie was merely wounded a few hours earlier; how could he now take the life of someone who had surrendered to him? But surrounding them both were groups of rough samurai who did not feel the same way, so for the sake of Atsumori's personal honour Naozane felt that it was he who should do the deed and then pray for his victim's rebirth in Paradise. So Naozane cut off Atsumori's head and became even more stricken with remorse when a flute fell out of the young man's sleeve. None of the rough eastern warriors, thought Naozane, could play the flute, and the mentally tortured Naozane eventually became a monk.

Ichinotani could easily have become the last battle of the Gempei War. Only the presence of the Taira boats prevented a massacre, but the escape of the survivors was by no means an orderly withdrawal. Instead we read of

The loss of young Taira Atsumori was the most tragic death to occur at the battle of Ichinotani. Here he appears in an effigy at Sumadera, the Buddhist temple built on the site of the battlefield.

In the garden of Sumadera the challenge made by Kumagai Naozane to Taira Atsumori is depicted using two fine statues. The gravel is raked to look like the surface of the sea.

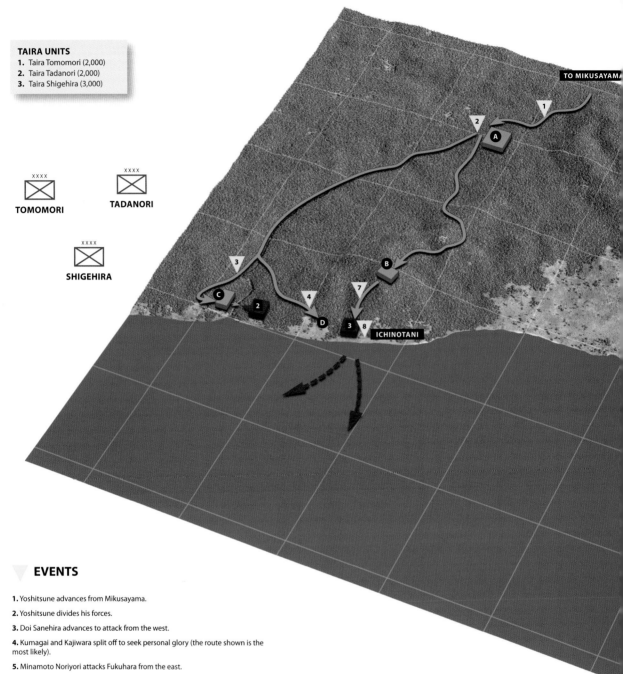

TAIRA UNITS
1. Taira Tomomori (2,000)
2. Taira Tadanori (2,000)
3. Taira Shigehira (3,000)

TO MIKUSAYAMA

XXXX
TOMOMORI

XXXX
TADANORI

XXXX
SHIGEHIRA

ICHINOTANI

EVENTS

1. Yoshitsune advances from Mikusayama.

2. Yoshitsune divides his forces.

3. Doi Sanehira advances to attack from the west.

4. Kumagai and Kajiwara split off to seek personal glory (the route shown is the most likely).

5. Minamoto Noriyori attacks Fukuhara from the east.

6. Noriyori advances through Fukuhara to Ichinotani.

7. Yoshitsune launches a rear attack on Ichinotani down the Hidoyorigoe.

8. Fighting continues on the beach as the Taira withdraw.

9. The Taira escape to Yashima.

THE BATTLE OF ICHINOTANI, 1184

Taira Munemori and the Emperor Antoku (with the crown jewels) had already departed Fukuhara, leaving others to defend Ichinotani. Yoshitsune and Noriyori planned a bold move to catch the Taira before they had a chance to take to the sea, dividing forces. Yoshitsune's surprise attack down the steep and rocky Hiyodorigoe behind Ichinotani pressed the Taira forces back to the beach, from which they made their escape. The locations of Fukuhara and the imperial palace are approximate.

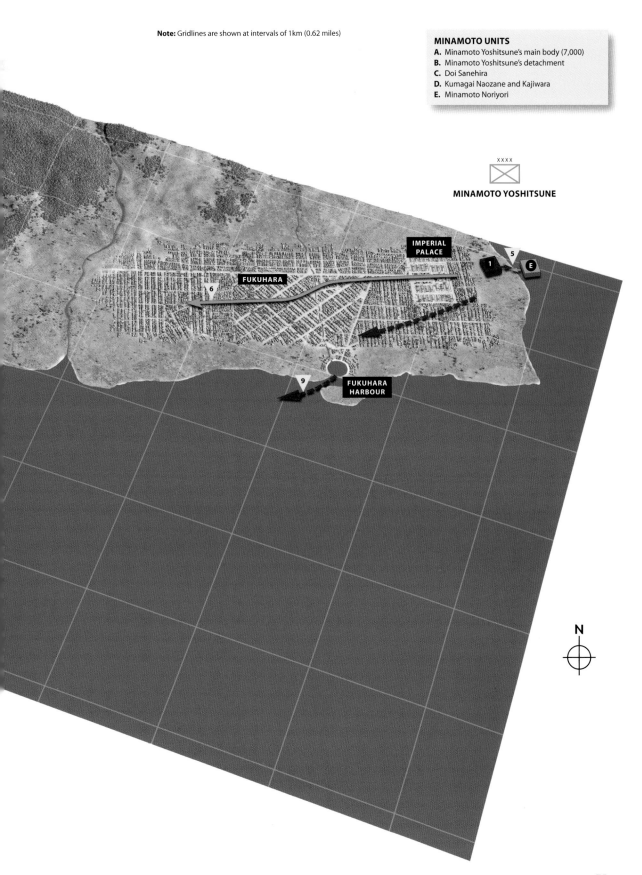

Note: Gridlines are shown at intervals of 1km (0.62 miles)

MINAMOTO UNITS
A. Minamoto Yoshitsune's main body (7,000)
B. Minamoto Yoshitsune's detachment
C. Doi Sanehira
D. Kumagai Naozane and Kajiwara
E. Minamoto Noriyori

xxxx

MINAMOTO YOSHITSUNE

IMPERIAL PALACE

FUKUHARA

FUKUHARA HARBOUR

N

75

The battle on the beach of Ichinotani became general as the Taira tried to escape to their ships.

boats capsizing, Minamoto samurai attempting to drag men out using rakes, and fights among the Taira to secure a place on board ship. Yet Yoshitsune lacked any means of pursuit, so that even though the Taira had been driven from Fukuhara forever, the emperor and the regalia were still in their possession and their command of the sea was still undisturbed. For this reason it would be a full six months before Yoshitsune would fight them again.

Minamoto Noriyori and the battle of Kojima

In spite of their huge defeat at Ichinotani the Taira were still in a strong position. Taira Tomomori, the ablest of the surviving Taira commanders, controlled Nagato province at the entrance to the Inland Sea, so even though the loss of Fukuhara meant that they were cut off from Kyoto, they could still reverse the overall position. A Taira naval victory like Mizushima against a Minamoto army enticed to the west would completely change the situation, and Tomomori was ready for them. The final result of course, would be a complete disaster for the Taira, and with the benefit of hindsight the narrative sequence of the battles of Ichinotani, Yashima and Dannoura fit neatly together. Straight after Ichinotani, however, the position was not in any way clear-cut.

Two factors that influenced the final phase of the Gempei War are frequently overlooked. The first is the gap of six months that passed between Ichinotani and Yashima; the second is that while Yoshitsune was engaged in the events that led to Yashima, his younger brother Noriyori was conducting a comparatively unglamorous campaign against the Taira along the *San'yōdō*. Only one battle was fought but Noriyori's expedition was to have a considerable influence on what was to follow. After the battle of Ichinotani Noriyori had returned to Kamakura, and following a necessary rest and regrouping Minamoto Yoritomo sent him back to join Yoshitsune with an order to vanquish the Taira. After being officially commissioned in this task by the Cloistered Emperor Go-Shirakawa, Noriyori left Kyoto on 8 October 1184. His ambitious objectives were first to secure Nagato province to control the Straits of Shimonoseki. He would then cross over to Kyūshū, subdue the Taira supporters there and take up a position in the Taira rear. Because of the Taira command of the sea the whole scheme had to be carried out overland as far as Nagato, so the Taira naturally harassed him at every turn. Noriyori defeated one of these thrusts at the battle of Kojima, also called Fujito (in modern Okayama city). The little island of Kojima was one more Taira outpost, and there Taira Tomomori attempted to stop Noriyori's advance. The Taira felt quite secure in their small fortress in the sea but Sasaki Moritsuna, one of the Minamoto commanders,

This rock within the garden of the Sanbō-In in Kyoto is the most curious memorial of the Gempei War. It is supposed to have been stained by the blood of the fisherman murdered by Sasaki Moritsuna at the battle of Kojima in 1185.

did some investigating. Moritsuna was the elder brother of Sasaki Takatsuna, who had won the race across the Uji River. He realised that the low tide might reveal a passable causeway, which he confirmed through a local fisherman, whom Moritsuna first rewarded and then killed lest his valuable intelligence be revealed. At dawn the following morning, 10 January 1185, Moritsuna emulated his brother's river crossing as he led his horsemen across the shallow waters. The Taira outpost was overrun, but Noriyori's force did not have any boats with which to pursue the Taira as they put to sea.

The combination of daring and callousness shown by Sasaki Moritsuna at Kojima would provide much future artistic inspiration. The Noh play *Fujito* has Moritsuna returning to the site of his triumph to be confronted by the dead fisherman's grieving mother and then by the ghost of his victim. More quietly dramatic is the story behind one of the stones in the garden of the Sanbō-In in Kyoto. This rock, which provides a focal point for the beautiful temple garden, was coveted by Toyotomi Hideyoshi, on whose behalf the garden was being created in 1597. Legend said that the rock had once lain beside the hidden causeway to Kojima and was stained by the blood of the murdered fisherman. It was transferred to the Sanbō-In and stands today as an unintended memorial to the Gempei War.

By his victory at Kojima and considerable dogged determination, Noriyori slowly prevailed against the Taira raiders and managed to make his way as far as Nagato by 13 February 1185. Here he came up against the territory controlled by Taira Tomomori, who was almost unassailable on Hikojima, the island that controlled the straits at the western entrance to the Inland Sea. Hikojima is now part of Shimonoseki city and is linked to it by two modern bridges. Unable to make it over to Kyūshū and faced by resistance and denial of supplies in Nagato, Noriyori's troops were forced back into the province of Suō. Food became so short there that his followers grew restive and mutinous, so with a supreme effort Noriyori assembled enough boats from local sympathisers for his army to cross from Suō to Bungo province in Kyūshū at a safe distance from the Taira. It was a much longer journey to make, and it turned out that his landfall in Bungo province promised little more in terms of provisions than had been provided by Suō, so the clamour for a return to Kamakura grew even louder.

Yoritomo, however, urged his brother to stand firm. This Noriyori agreed to do, and his brave decision turned out to be decisive in the subsequent victory of Dannoura, because the presence on Kyūshū of his disaffected army, whose wretched condition cannot have been appreciated in any way by the Taira, was to have a considerable effect on the battle. The Taira had wanted to move across to the greater security of Kyūshū. It was the supposed threat from Noriyori that made Taira Munemori abandon that plan. Instead Minamoto Noriyori's army acted as a containing force that exerted an influence out of all proportion to its actual physical state. Their mere presence to the rear of the Taira persuaded their enemies to stay on Hikojima and supposedly enjoy the safety that control of the straits and their naval superiority guaranteed. The eventual Minamoto triumph at Dannoura involved destroying both of these illusions. As for their safety, Noriyori had made a huge contribution by confining the Taira to this small area, but nothing could have been achieved if the Minamoto had not also been able to match the Taira in their naval capacity, and here again Noriyori had played a part. His slow but secure military successes on his march along the *San'yōdō* had persuaded local warrior bands from Suō to join the Minamoto cause. They brought men, but they also brought ships.

Yoshitsune and the battle of Yashima

We will return to the details of this development later, because in between the encounters at Kojima and Dannoura one other great battle was fought at the Taira base at Yashima in Sanuki province on Shikoku. Yashima lies to the east of modern Takamatsu city and is dominated by an easily defensible volcanic plateau that was a separate island in 1185, but the Taira base was not on the top of a mountain. Once again the need for seagoing access predominated, so the Yashima headquarters lay on the strait between Yashima and the mainland of Shikoku. As *Heike Monogatari* puts it, 'They thought they would be safe, trusting in the mountains and the sea.'

The plateau of Yashima as seen from the now reclaimed area of land that was sea at the time of the famous battle of 1185.

The site of the battle of Yashima looking down from Yashimadera, the temple built on top of the plateau of the once-separated island. The battle was fought in the shallows between the island and the mainland.

Minamoto Yoshitsune had used the time since Ichinotani to fit out a fleet. Quite how he achieved this is not recorded, but it is likely that several local lords moved over to the Minamoto side after Ichinotani. The boats thus collected were assembled at the port of Watanabe for the first Minamoto seaborne expedition, a prospect that filled some of his army with dread. Kajiwara Kagetoki, the man who had saved Yoritomo's life after Ishibashiyama, was particularly critical about the design of Yoshitsune's boats and argued very strongly that because of the type of combat in which they would be engaged, a set of oars should be mounted in the bows as well as the stern so that the boats could pull back speedily. It was a sensible tactical suggestion, but Yoshitsune angrily rejected it out of hand. He had no intention of retreating, tactically or not.

Before the battle of Yashima, Kajiwara Kagetoki infuriated Yoshitsune by suggesting that extra oars should be placed in the bows of their boats to aid withdrawal. Yoshitsune said no, insisting that he would never retreat.

Even though the Minamoto now had a navy of sorts, Yoshitsune did not intend to engage the Taira at Yashima by sea. By contrast, he wished to avoid it, so the boats were simply a means of transport to the dry land of Shikoku and an overland raid like Ichinotani. Their planned route to Yashima was therefore an indirect one south of the island of Awaji to land on Shikoku some distance to the east. Yoshitsune set sail on 22 March in the teeth of a furious gale which he hoped would add an element of surprise to their attack, but his samurai did not share this enthusiasm and some had to be forced aboard at sword point. They sailed overnight and landed at a place called Katsuura. As the name means 'victory beach', it was of course taken as a good omen. On disembarking they saddled up and rode off to deal with a minor Taira outpost nearby, then headed overnight for Yashima.

The surprise of their arrival cannot be compared in any way to the descent of Hiyodorigoe at Ichinotani, but their means of introduction was the same. Anything that could be burned was set on fire and under the cover of smoke the Minamoto samurai charged down towards the sea. Once again the emperor was hustled onto a boat, but instead of heading directly for the open sea and escape the Taira fleet gathered in the narrow channel between Yashima and the mainland, taunting the Minamoto to fight them at a disadvantage. As the water was shallow, the Minamoto were able to wade out on horseback and engage in mounted archery, and because of this the Yashima narrative contains more examples of challenges given and received

Mionoya Jūrō escaped from being killed in single combat when the neckpiece of his helmet, which his opponent was pulling, came apart at the lacing.

On this lacquered tray is shown the scene at the battle of Yashima when Minamoto Yoshitsune risked his life to retrieve his bow from the sea. He was small of stature and his bow was of a comparatively short length, so he did not want to be mocked for his lack of physical strength.

by samurai archers than at Ichinotani. *Heike Monogatari* also reveals that Yoshitsune was surrounded by a group of bodyguards, four of whom made up his *shi-tennō* ('four heavenly kings'), together with the famous Benkei. Taira Noritsune managed to get Yoshitsune within archery range, but these men closed around him, so that even though Noritsune brought down ten Minamoto samurai, he could not touch Yoshitsune. One of his victims was Yoshitsune's bodyguard Satō Tsuginobu, who received an arrow from Noritsune that hit a weak point between the helmet and shoulder plates and pierced him through from his left shoulder to his right armpit.

Another section of the painted screen at Yashimadera showing the battle of Yashima.

The most celebrated incident of skill with bow and arrow at Yashima occurred during a lull in the fighting when the Taira hung a fan from the mast of one of their ships and invited the Minamoto to shoot it down, hoping thereby to make them lose face. A young samurai called Nasu Yoichi Munetaka took up the challenge and hit the fan with his first arrow, even though he was on horseback in the water and the boat he was aiming at was rocking on the waves some distance away. Yoichi's feat did wonders for the morale of the Minamoto, but not all the Taira were intimidated to stay within the security of their boats. One small group bravely rode to the shore and challenged the Minamoto to single combat. Among them was Mionoya Jūrō of Musashi, who had his horse shot from under him:

> The rider at once threw his left leg over the animal and vaulted down to the right, drawing his sword to continue the fight, but when he saw the warrior behind the shield come to meet him flourishing a huge *naginata*, he knew that his own small sword would be useless, and blew on a conch and retreated. The other immediately followed him, and it looked as though he would cut him down with his *naginata*, but instead of doing so, gripping the *naginata* under his left arm, he tried to seize Mionoya no Jūrō by the neckpiece of his helmet with his right hand. Three times Mionoya eluded his grasp, but at the fourth attempt his opponent held on. For a moment he could do nothing, but then, giving a sudden violent wrench, the neckpiece parted where it joined the helmet, and Mionoya escaped and hid behind his four companions to recover his breath.

After a few further scuffles the brave Taira samurai beat a retreat back to their ships, at which the Minamoto rode as close as they could and fought among the shallows. The Taira on board one of the ships tried to seize hold of Yoshitsune with rakes and hooks, causing him to drop his bow and put himself at some personal risk in his efforts to retrieve it. Yoshitsune clearly felt that his reputation as an archer, and therefore as a samurai, would be undermined if his enemies realised that he lacked the physical strength to draw a large bow. When night fell the Taira were still lying off shore, so the Minamoto withdrew and took up a position on the plateau of Yashima from where they had a view of the strait. They also made use of a pond fed by a mountain stream that allowed them to wash the salt water and blood from their armour. As dawn broke, the Taira withdrew to the bay of Shido so Yoshitsune led a pursuit along the coast on horseback. At this the Taira finally sailed away for the safety of the Inland Sea and their refuge on Hikoshima. Once again their command of the sea had allowed them to avoid a decisive defeat.

Taira Tomomori and the battle of Dannoura

At Yashima the Taira had escaped for a second time, but their nemesis lay not far into the future at Dannoura, the battle whereby the Gempei War came to an end with one of the most decisive and remarkable conflicts in Japanese history. Its decisiveness lay in the utter destruction inflicted upon the Taira, while its remarkable nature lay in the final and complete reversal of the balance of superiority between land and sea warfare enjoyed by the two rivals. At the battle of Yashima scarcely a month earlier Yoshitsune had tried to avoid a naval action at all costs; now he chose to engage the Taira on what appeared to be a watery battlefield of their own choosing. Yet even though

Dannoura is one of the best-known battles in Japanese history, there remains a mystery over how Yoshitsune achieved such a staggering victory. Very few firm details are known about what happened, particularly concerning the events that occurred prior to the engagement surrounding his acquisition of a superior fleet.

It is quite clear that during the time between Yashima and Dannoura a transformation took place in the Taira–Minamoto naval balance. This was partly due to Noriyori's success on land and the resulting pledges of support noted above. A similar view was taken by the lords on Shikoku who had witnessed Yoshitsune's victory at Yashima, and because of their locations on the Inland Sea all these new sympathisers brought ships with them. *Azuma Kagami* relates how on 24 March 1185 Kōno Michinobu came to Yoshitsune with 30 boats. The following day Kajiwara Kagetoki acquired 140 more from unnamed sources, and on 22 April – the day before Yoshitsune set sail for Dannoura – a certain Gorō Masatoshi, described as a *funadokoro* (commissioner for boats), contributed 'several tens' of vessels. In one case divine intervention played its part. *Heike Monogatari* tells of a former Taira ally called Tanzō witnessing a cockfight at a Shintō shrine where seven white cocks defeated seven red cocks. This was regarded as a good omen, so he joined the Minamoto along with 2,000 men and 200 boats.

As a result of these additions the Minamoto fleet outnumbered the Taira by the time of the battle. Most accounts say that Yoshitsune commanded around 700 vessels, although *Azuma Kagami* puts the figure at 840. The Taira, formerly the masters of the seas, had no more than 500 ships, and not all of their commanders could be relied upon. Crucially, a certain Taguchi Shigeyoshi had taken part in the flight from Yashima to the west and had left his son behind

The site of the battle of Dannoura is marked by this large statue of Taira Tomomori holding an anchor to aid his suicide by drowning. In the distance is the modern suspension bridge that crosses the Straits of Shimonoseki at its narrowest point.

to safeguard their lands in Iyo province. The son surrendered to Yoshitsune and was persuaded to write to his father urging him to change sides when conflict was rejoined. It is clear that some within the Taira command were very suspicious of Shigeyoshi because when Taira Tomomori prepared his fleet for the contest at Dannoura, he urged Munemori to have him put to death. Munemori refused to listen and placed Shigeyoshi in the front line.

It is not known for certain where Yoshitsune's fleet embarked. It is unlikely to have been as far away as Shikoku because they were spotted by Taira scouts on the same day and their advance was reported to Hikojima, so they probably set sail from somewhere in Suō. The most likely place is the island of Ōshima, because that is where a further defector called Miura Yoshizumi joined Yoshitsune. His presence was most welcome because he was familiar with the Straits of Shimonoseki, so Yoshitsune assigned him to lead the vanguard and act as guide. He led the Minamoto fleet to the area of sea that lay just to the south of the small uninhabited islands of Kanjushima and Manjushima. There they made ready. The Taira set off immediately to meet them, proceeding north-eastwards through the Straits of Shimonoseki. Taira Tomomori was in supreme command, accompanied by just about every other surviving Taira leader. *Azuma Kagami* also names Yamaga Hidetō who commanded a squadron and the presence of the *Matsuura-tō*. *Tō* in this context can be understood as 'gang' so they were probably seamen from the Matsuura area of Kyūshū who led lives on the edge of the law. The Kumano and Iyo 'fleets' on the Minamoto side probably had a similar piratical background.

The modern visitor to the site of Dannoura can easily appreciate the strategic position of the narrow strait and the relative closeness of Honshū and Kyūshū. The island of Hikojima has previously been referred to, but beside the

Small Taira boats at the battle of Dannoura are shown on this painted screen at the Watanabe Museum in Tottori.

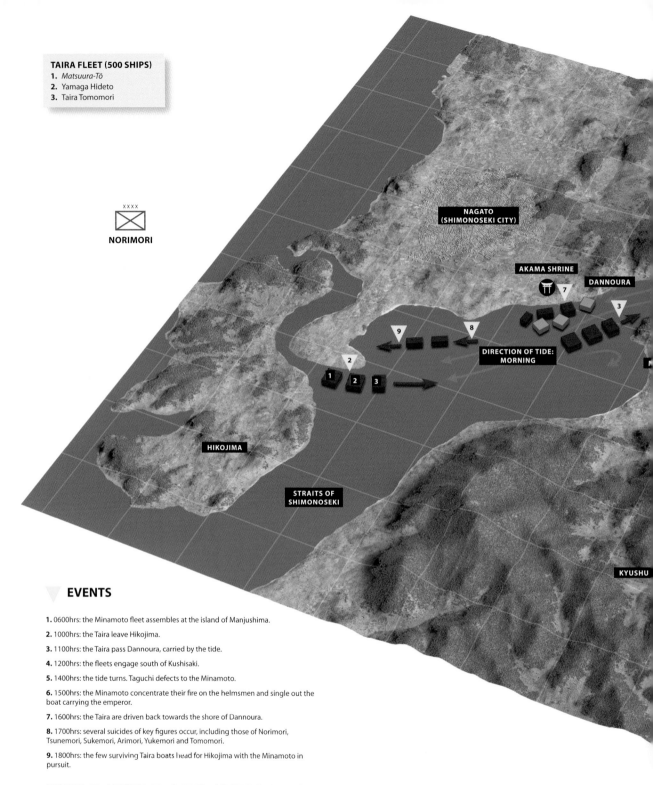

TAIRA FLEET (500 SHIPS)
1. *Matsuura-Tō*
2. Yamaga Hideto
3. Taira Tomomori

XXXX
NORIMORI

NAGATO
(SHIMONOSEKI CITY)

AKAMA SHRINE

DANNOURA

DIRECTION OF TIDE:
MORNING

HIKOJIMA

STRAITS OF
SHIMONOSEKI

KYUSHU

▼ EVENTS

1. 0600hrs: the Minamoto fleet assembles at the island of Manjushima.

2. 1000hrs: the Taira leave Hikojima.

3. 1100hrs: the Taira pass Dannoura, carried by the tide.

4. 1200hrs: the fleets engage south of Kushisaki.

5. 1400hrs: the tide turns. Taguchi defects to the Minamoto.

6. 1500hrs: the Minamoto concentrate their fire on the helmsmen and single out the boat carrying the emperor.

7. 1600hrs: the Taira are driven back towards the shore of Dannoura.

8. 1700hrs: several suicides of key figures occur, including those of Norimori, Tsunemori, Sukemori, Arimori, Yukemori and Tomomori.

9. 1800hrs: the few surviving Taira boats head for Hikojima with the Minamoto in pursuit.

THE BATTLE OF DANNOURA, 25 APRIL 1185

The Taira planned to use the strong current in the Straits of Shimonoseki to their advantage, launching their attack with the tide in their favour. As the two fleets engaged, the rival boats became completely mixed up, and fierce fighting developed with bows, swords and *naginata*. Taguchi Shigeyoshi's treachery would turn the tide of battle in favour of the Minamoto, and bring about the death of the young emperor Antoku.

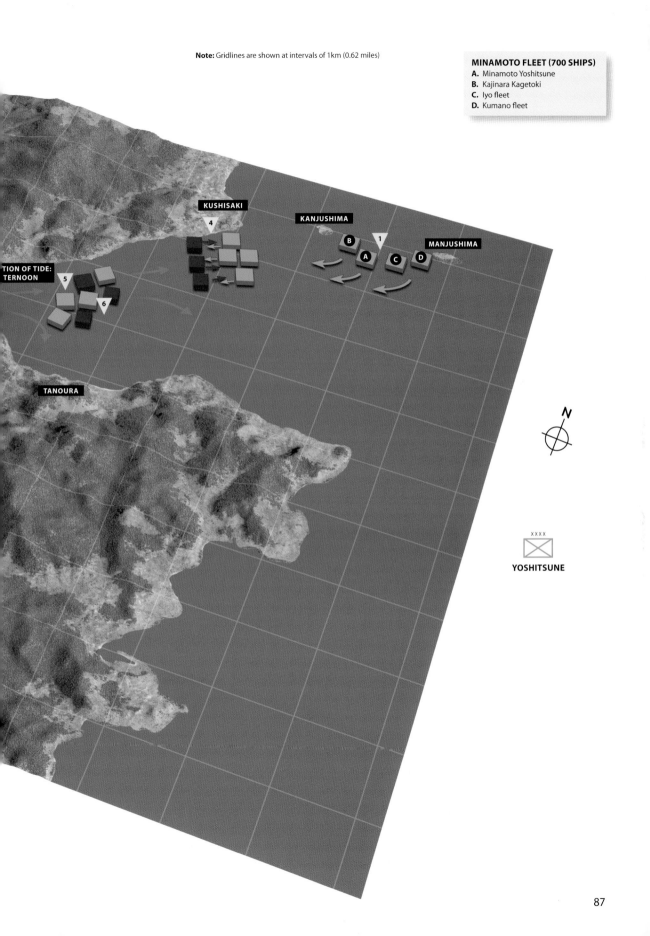

Note: Gridlines are shown at intervals of 1km (0.62 miles)

MINAMOTO FLEET (700 SHIPS)
A. Minamoto Yoshitsune
B. Kajinara Kagetoki
C. Iyo fleet
D. Kumano fleet

KUSHISAKI

KANJUSHIMA

MANJUSHIMA

TION OF TIDE:
TERNOON

TANOURA

N

XXXX
YOSHITSUNE

beach of Dannoura the sea passage is the narrowest of all. It is dominated by a mountain on each side and crossed by a modern suspension bridge. Beneath the sea at Moji is a 700m-long pedestrian tunnel and a rail tunnel completed in recent years that conveys the *Kyūshū Shinkansen*, the high-speed 'Bullet Train'. A much longer visit would be required to appreciate the other crucial factor about the Straits of Shimonoseki. This is the fierce tidal current that alternates its flow in and out of the Inland Sea. It was a feature with which the Taira were very familiar and planned to use to their advantage, because while the Minamoto held their position to the south of Kanjushima and Manjushima, the Taira fleet launched their attack with the tide in their favour and came bearing down upon the Minamoto, carried easily along by the rapid current. They had divided their attacking fleet into three, the better to penetrate the Minamoto lines and gain a quick victory before the tide turned.

By about 1100hrs the two fleets had engaged and arrows began to hit their marks. Mindful of the need for a boat's manoeuvrability (a matter he had once scorned), Yoshitsune ordered his archers to concentrate on the Taira helmsmen and steerers, and as the fleets closed, bows were given to attendants and swords or *naginata* unsheathed. By midday the rival boats were completely mixed up. Any remaining archery duels were now at very close quarters and the forward boats were beginning to experience *yoroi-gumi*. Sensing that the battle was not going their way, Taira Noritsune was determined to take Yoshitsune's head and fought his way on to the Minamoto commander's boat. So fierce was this personal assault that Yoshitsune was forced to leap onto another boat while two samurai grabbed Noritsune. He kicked one overboard and seized the other two, one under each arm, then leapt into the sea to commit suicide.

Then two things happened. First, the tide began to turn at about 1500hrs, and although this would in time drive the Taira back along the strait to their defeat, it was at present of much less significance than the act of treason now committed by Taguchi Shigeyoshi. As his son had assured Minamoto Yoshitsune, Shigeyoshi came over to the Minamoto side when battle was joined. In addition to the surprise and the increase in fighting strength that his defection provided, Shigeyoshi also arrived with some vital information. Before setting out from Hikojima the Taira had made the decision to take the child emperor Antoku with them on board ship. No doubt this was done because it was believed that he would be safer there than left behind with a guard on Hikojima, where Noriyori's supposedly strong army could capture him

On this woodblock print Minamoto Yoshitsune jumps into an adjacent boat to avoid the attentions of Taira Noritsune, who was determined to take his head.

while the battle progressed. It was still a terrible risk to take, so to increase his security Antoku had not been placed on board the large ornate Chinese-style flagship against which the Minamoto had been mounting their main attacks. Instead he was on a small boat indistinguishable from all the others. As part of his treacherous act Taguchi Shigeyoshi disclosed to the Minamoto which vessel it was. From that moment on the Minamoto turned their forces on to the correct target and the battle was effectively lost. Their concentration of fire on the rowers and the helmsmen also meant that many Taira ships were now out of control and beginning to drift back helplessly with the tide. All seemed lost, and there was only one course of action available to keep the emperor and the regalia from falling into Minamoto hands:

> Then the Nii Dono (Antoku's grandmother), who had already resolved what she would do, donning a double outer dress of dark grey mourning colour, and tucking up the long skirts of her glossy silk *hakama*, put the Sacred Jewel under her arm, and the Sacred Sword in her girdle, and taking the emperor in her arms, spoke thus, 'In the depths of the ocean we have a capital', and sank with him beneath the waves.

A few minutes later the Sacred Mirror almost joined them. The wife of Taira Shigehira was about to jump into the sea when an arrow pinned her robe to the side of the boat, forcing her to drop the casket she was carrying:

> She stumbled and fell, whereupon the Genji soldiers seized her and held her back. Then one of them wrenched off the lock of the casket to open it, when suddenly his eyes were darkened and blood poured from his nose. At this Taira Dainagon Tokitada no Kyo, who had been captured alive and was standing nearby, exclaimed, 'Hold! That is the Holy *Naishi Dokoro*, the Sacred Mirror that no profane eye must behold!' Whereat the soldiers were awe-stricken and trembled with fear.

LEFT
Taira Noritsune prepares to commit suicide with a Minamoto samurai under each arm. Note that the print maker has him standing on the shore rather than a boat.

RIGHT
When the battle of Dannoura was known to be lost, Emperor Antoku's grandmother prepared to drown him to prevent him falling into the hands of the Minamoto. The scene is depicted here on a life-sized diorama at the Heike Monogatari Museum in Takamatsu.

Wearing two suits of armour and weighed down by an anchor, Taira Tomomori commits suicide by drowning.

The Sacred Sword was lost forever and the present one is a replica. Of the other three items the jewel was recovered and the mirror provided its own defence mechanism as noted above. As the tide grew in strength, the Taira ships were driven towards the shore of Dannoura. Although he is nowhere mentioned, it is more than likely that Minamoto Noriyori had stationed his bedraggled army on the southern (Kyūshū) side of the straits, making the Taira think they were completely surrounded with no hope left. Realising that the battle was lost, many of the Taira samurai followed Noritsune's example and committed suicide by jumping into the sea. *Heike Monogatari* notes that Taira Norimori, Tsunemori, Sukemori, Arimori and Yukemori all tied anchors to themselves to guarantee a death by drowning. The cowardly Munemori hesitated, standing on the gunwale of his ship, until a furious Taira samurai pushed him into the water. His son Kiyomune jumped in after him. Ise Yoshimori then dragged Taira Kiyomune out of the sea using a rake, and Taira Munemori allowed himself to be pulled out also and taken alive. Others were made of sterner stuff:

Seeing this Hida no Saburōemon Kagetsune, foster brother of Munemori, jumped into Yoshimori's boat and aimed a blow at him with his sword, shouting, 'Who are you to take my lord captive?' But Yoshimori's page, perceiving his master's danger, thrust himself in between to intercept the blow, which fell full on his helmet and split it open. A second blow cut off the faithful page's head.

This little shrine on the shore of Dannoura marks the site of a freshwater spring that becomes saline at high tide. That was the nasty surprise that awaited the Taira samurai who managed to escape from the sea.

The final suicide was that of Taira Tomomori, who put on two suits of armour to weigh his body down and also held on to an anchor. *Heike Monogatari* then provides the visual image that was to become the enduring memory of Dannoura. 'Now the whole sea was red with the banners and insignia that they tore off and cut away … while the white breakers that rolled up on the beach were dyed a scarlet colour'. A few Taira samurai did manage to escape and make it to the northern shore where, parched by thirst, they found a pond of fresh water, but the rising tide soon made it salty. Some boats probably made it back to Hikojima, and these survivors were to provide the later legends of 'Heike

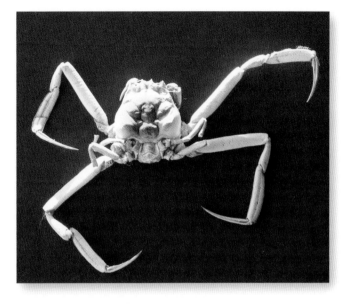

This is one of the Heike crabs which live in the sea off Dannoura. They are supposed to contain the spirit of a dead warrior, and a fierce samurai face may be discerned upon their shells.

villages', isolated hamlets in the mountains where survivors of the Taira lived anonymously for generations. Beside the beach of Dannoura the massacre was almost total, and one other powerful legend associated with Dannoura is that of the so-called Heike crabs who live in the vicinity. Their shells have the appearance of the face of a dead samurai. Legend grew that this was because the spirits of dead Taira samurai lived inside them. Other ghost stories developed that told of dead warriors rising from the waves to attack any ships containing the Minamoto who passed through the Straits of Shimonoseki, a theme that found expression in the Noh theatre. Nowadays the graves of the Taira lords who perished at Dannoura are located at the rear of the Akamagū, the shrine on the shore that was raised to comfort the spirit of Emperor Antoku. This place provides the focus for memorialisation of the great battle with which the Gempei War came to its tremendous end.

The graves of the Taira leaders who died at Dannoura are to be found at the rear of the Akamagū, the shrine erected to comfort the spirit of Emperor Antoku.

AFTERMATH

YOSHITSUNE'S FLIGHT AND THE BATTLE OF KOROMOGAWA

There was one very important military aftermath to the Gempei War. Yoritomo's victory had been delivered by Yoshitsune, but the jealous Minamoto Yoritomo then turned against his brother. Yoshitsune first sought sanctuary in Yoshino. Fighting beside him was Satō Tadanobu, whose elder

The Benkei-dō in Hiraizumi marks the location of the battle of Koromogawa in 1189 where Yoshitsune and Benkei were both killed. In the foreground is an effigy of the famous warrior monk. Yoshitsune sits at the rear.

brother Tsuginobu had been killed at the battle of Yashima. While Yoshitsune was passing through the mountains, his party was surprised by Yoritomo's samurai, and Tadanobu fought a rearguard action dressed as Yoshitsune while his master made his escape. The ploy was successful, but Tadanobu was eventually captured and put to death.

Yoshitsune then fled to the north of Japan and found sanctuary with the Ōshū Fujiwara who had looked after him during his previous exile. It was within their territory in Tōhoku (north-east Japan) that he fought his last battle at Koromogawa. The Ōshū Fujiwara enjoyed such independence in their 'Little Kyoto' in Hiraizumi that they could contemplate challenging the might of Yoritomo. Faced by the advance north of Yoritomo's army in 1189, Fujiwara Kunihira resorted to a bold defensive measure by excavating a triple embankment earthwork with a double ditch over a distance of about 3km between the mountain of Atsukashiyama and the Atsukashi River in what is now Fukushima Prefecture. Although it was reinforced with watchtowers and defended by *oyumi* (siege crossbows) for the last time in Japanese history, it succeeded in stalling the Minamoto advance for only a short time. *Azuma Kagami* tells us that during an attack on one of the strong points along the line Yoritomo's men took 18 heads in spite of deadly arrows from an *oyumi*. Fujiwara Kunihira was killed in the fighting, and not long afterwards his family's illustrious refugee Yoshitsune was finally defeated at the battle of Koromogawa. Benkei was with him to the last, and the epic *Yoshitsune* contains a vivid description of Benkei's last stand, pierced with arrows and yet still defiant against the advancing Taira. It was only when a horseman galloped by and caught him with a blow that toppled him over that everyone realised he was already dead. Yoshitsune then retired and committed suicide.

YORITOMO AND THE SHOGUNATE

So complete was Yoritomo's destruction of his rivals and so total was his control of the emperor that he could contemplate reshaping the way Japan was governed in a way that Taira Kiyomori could never have achieved. Yoritomo's new regime is often said to be the replacement of imperial authority with the emperor relegated to the level of a figurehead, but that had already happened with the cloistered system and the deaths of several imperial claimants. The change that Yoritomo wrought was a real revolution. The Taira had ruled through the existing institutions because they controlled the imperial bureaucracy. Minamoto Yoritomo supplanted them, and no one had ever tried that in Japanese history. He already had a working model back in Kamakura in the form of his *Samurai-dokoro* that controlled the eastern lords who had pledged allegiance to him. Yoritomo's success in the war was effectively a victory of Eastern Japan over Western Japan, so he reinvented the *Samurai-dokoro* on a nationwide scale as the *bakufu*, the 'government behind the curtain'. The title he took in 1192 was *Sei-i-ta Shogun* ('Barbarian-quelling Commander-in-Chief'). This was an ancient temporary commission that emperors had bestowed upon their champions who had ridden off to conquer rebels and advance the frontiers of civilised Japan. That temporary commission from the emperor now became a permanent one and Minamoto Yoritomo became Japan's first Shogun.

He did not live long to enjoy his power. Minamoto Yoritomo died in 1199 following a fall from his horse. His death threw the Shogunate into confusion, and because his son and heir Yoriie was only 8 years old, Yoritomo's widow Masako took over as regent. When Yoriie eventually became Shogun, he was forced to retire and was murdered. His younger brother Sanetomo then took over, but he too was assassinated. The instigators of these deeds were Masako's family of the Hōjō. They were to rule Japan for a further century, but only as regents, not as shoguns. That title stayed within the Minamoto clan, whose extended lineage would one day revive the post and then maintain it over many centuries. The last Shogun only abdicated in 1868, a testimony to the allure of the post that had been forged in Japan's great Gempei War.

FURTHER READING

The version of *Heike Monogatari* that I have used here is the translation by A. L. Sadler that was published by the Asiatic Society of Japan in 1918 and 1921. This is my personal favourite and is not readily available, but there are several excellent modern translations in print. A selective translation of *Azuma Kagami* appears in *The Founding of the Kamakura Shogunate* by Minoru Shinoda (1960). For a detailed account of how the samurai are presented in the *gunkimono* see H. P. Varley's *Warriors of Japan as Portrayed in the War Tales* (1994). William Wayne Farris' *Heavenly Warriors: The Evolution of Japan's Military, 500–1300* (1992) contains a very good summary of the Gempei War and contemporary military technology, as does Karl Friday's *Samurai: Warfare and the State in Early Medieval Japan* (2004). The Japanese publication *Gempei Kassen Jinbutsuden* (2004) is a superbly illustrated guide to the personalities of the Gempei War.

INDEX